Get Cast

Book More Acting Work By

Thinking "Outside the Industry"

Start booking roles of substance that will challenge you, get you in front of more people, and take your acting career to new heights - whether you're just starting out or a fully-seasoned actor.

Martin Bentsen

Actor Marketing Coach & Founder of City Headshots

DISCLAIMER AND/OR LEGAL NOTICES:

The information presented herein represents the view of the author as of the date of publication. Because of the rate with which conditions change, the author reserves the right to alter and update his opinions based on the new conditions. The book is for informational purposes only. While every attempt has been made to verify the information provided in this eBook, neither the author nor his affiliates/partners assume any responsibility for errors, inaccuracies or omissions. Any slights of people or organizations are unintentional. If advice concerning legal or related matters is needed, the services of a fully qualified professional should be sought. This book is not intended for use as a source of legal advice.

How to Use this Book

I wrote this book as a simple, step by step system you can follow to move your acting career forward rapidly.

The steps have worked for many actors, helping them book Broadway and recurring television roles, land agents, and even get featured in *Backstage Magazine.*

Each section can be read separately as its own resource, but I recommend you first read through the whole book from start to finish to get a grasp on the system as a whole.

I also wrote this book to be *timeless.*

The world changes so fast that within the next 5-10 years, the current most used social media platforms and websites will probably no longer be popular. Simple tactics that work well now might not make any sense soon!

Therefore, this book discusses strategy, psychology, and action steps you can take to move your acting career forward, but does not discuss social media, technology, and other very specific tools you can make use of.

But I want to make sure you still have access to the most effective, up-to-date resources. That's why I set up a members-only website for this book that I keep up to date.

Lifetime access is included with the purchase of this book. All you have to do to join is visit the link below:

www.martinbentsen.com/get-cast

Here are just a few of the resources I've included (note that these might change over time as we keep the pages up to date):

- Special interviews with industry professionals, including casting directors, agents, managers, and successful actors

- Mailing lists and how to use them to build a fan base

- How to join the different acting unions, and when to join and not to join

- Sample cover letter templates that have been tested and vastly improve your chances of getting an interview with an agency

- Social media marketing and building an online following

- And much more...

I hope you enjoy this book!

— Martin Bentsen

Who is This Book For?

This book is for any actor that wants to learn how to surpass the competition by being systematic about their career.

Most artists (actors, photographers, painters, etc.) are not systematic in how they approach the business side of their work. They spend most of their time refining their craft but avoid spending time on marketing themselves!

Actors want their voice heard and would love to get in front of more people, but many are either unwilling or don't understand how to do what's required to position themselves where they can be seen.

This is not their fault. The industry and many of those in it still recommend the same advice to actors - get a great headshot and reel, build your resume, find an agent, and keep submitting. Get on social media and "build your network." If you do all this, supposedly you'll eventually start to book bigger roles and build a following.

While this advice might have been valid years ago, the truth is with the advent of the internet and the ease with which actors can submit themselves for projects, there are infinitely more people trying to become actors these days, and because of the increased competition, it's next to impossible to move ahead without being highly strategic.

This book is for the actors who are willing to do the hard work and thinking necessary to build the career they dream of. This book is for actors who are open to trying something new and stepping out of their comfort zone. If you're open to looking at your career from a new perspective, this book is for you.

This book is NOT for actors who want to become famous in six months. There is no way to sidestep hard and consistent work, and anyone who promises otherwise is probably lying. But this book *will* show you a clear path to getting booked solid with work you love. And it will show you how to get there much sooner than you think:

- Want to perform on Broadway? This book will increase your chances drastically.

- Want to land a recurring or series regular role on a major television show? The strategy is here.

- Want to be cast as the lead in a feature film? It's completely possible.

Do you think those bullets sound crazy? Or like scams? Well they're not, I assure you. With consistent work and a little out-of-the-box thinking, they're much closer to becoming a reality than you think. Just ask my one-on-one coaching clients:

- **Mya Carter**, a highly talented actress without professional credits, decided to work with me with the goal of getting booked in a television show. She'd been working hard towards that goal for two years with no success. Within less than two weeks of our first call (where we discussed just 5% of what's in this book), she landed a supporting role in *Law and Order* for a highly-paid, multi-day shoot.

- **Zariah Cain** was just 13 years old with very few credits and connections. She had been needing an agent to book professional film and television roles. Within six weeks of starting with me she got an offer and signed with a great agency. Her career has been moving forward consistently and she feels much more focused now.

- **One of my clients (asked to stay anonymous)** had always wanted a job on Broadway, but had struggled to get one for over seven years. He hired me, we implemented just 15% of what's in this book, and in less than a month, he got an offer! A month after that he made his Broadway debut in Disney's *Frozen*.

So is this book for you? Well, if you're willing to put in some hard, focused work and you want to land the role of your dreams, I think it's safe to say you'll find what you're looking for within these pages.

The real question is, will you follow through and put in the work necessary?

Who Am I?

Throughout my twenties, I was frantic. Obsessive. Crazy. All I wanted was success. I wanted to become known. I wanted a small amount of fame and a big amount of money. Or a big amount of fame and a BIGGER amount of money! Maybe that was just the millennial in me speaking?

Anyway, as a photographer, I lived a life outside the boundaries and expectations of, how should I say... "normal" society. I could press snooze as many times as I wanted and binge watch *Breaking Bad* whenever there were no clients around.

I was making good money, had numerous clients, and was fairly happy. Or so I thought...

Here's the thing... Don't you hate it when you're feeling stressed about something and everyone around you says, "Hey, you're doing well, you should be happy!"

No. Stop talking to me. YOU DON'T GET IT!

Deep down I knew I could be doing more.

I stayed at that level for a year, doing the same kinds of projects, over and over again. And then came two years. And before I knew it, I realized I had been stuck at a plateau for over FIVE YEARS, lying to myself about my success, and trying to convince myself that I was some amazing business owner, when in reality I was still doing exactly the same work and earning the same money, but with more staff to pay!!!

I was mad. Why was it so hard? Was there some secret formula out there that could get me out of this trap? Or is it actually not possible to become wealthy, successful, and well-known unless you're one of the lucky few born into it?

Hmmmm...

I realized something needed to change.

So I asked myself... "Was becoming rich and famous what I really wanted?" What kind of absurd, unspecific, and quite frankly, selfish goal was that?

I thought about it and realized that wanting fame would never get me there. Wanting fame was exactly what was keeping me stuck. Wanting success for its own sake is useless because it's not sustainable and it's self-focused.

If there's one lesson I've learned over the past decade running my business, it's this: The only way to move beyond the realm of "good enough" is to ask yourself the following question:

"How can I go about helping and serving others at the deepest level and in a way that will truly change their lives?"

Many of the actors I'd shot headshots for would remark how helpful I'd been, and how the "outside-the-industry" marketing strategies I suggested helped them land an agent or book a role faster than they expected.

And that's when I realized exactly what needed to change:

I needed to turn what I loved doing most - helping actors move their careers forward - into a business.

And so I've done that now. It took me ten years to figure it out. But I'm passionate about my work again. I'm staying up late into the night answering all kinds of great emails from actors who read and engage with my articles. My business is growing. I'm waking up extremely early without my alarm again!

And best of all, I'm actually having a genuine impact on the lives of the actors I work with.

My biggest goal? To one day end the cliche of The Starving Artist.

Author's Biography

Martin Bentsen has spoken numerous times at *New York University*, has run educational seminars at *Actor's Connection* and *The Actor's Green Room* on branding and marketing strategies for performers, and works as a marketing coach helping actors achieve their biggest goals. He is a member of both the National Association of Sales Professionals and Sales & Marketing Executives

International, two highly acclaimed marketing organizations in the United States.

Martin graduated in 2011 with honors from NYU's Tisch School of the Arts with a focus on film directing. In 2009, he founded City Headshots®, which, according to Yelp, is ranked the top headshot studio in all of New York City. As of 2019, City Headshots employs 8 people and has locations in New York, Denver, Chicago, and Philadelphia. Some of City Headshots' repeat clients include well known companies such as *Facebook* and *American Express*, and some of its photos have been featured in *The New York Times* and *The Wall Street Journal*.

As a filmmaker and entrepreneur who has written four feature-length films, produced, cast, and directed two of them, and grown a company from zero to over 150 clients per month, Martin not only understands the intricacies of marketing and finding an audience, but also what it takes for actors to successfully navigate the casting world and make themselves memorable.

Table of Contents

Part 1: Change Your Thinking

The most important part of being successful in any industry is thinking differently than those around you.

It can be tempting to want to think and act the same as everyone else because it feels safer, but won't that lead you to the same outcome? And if most other actors feel stuck or overwhelmed, do you want to experience that too?

The first section of this book is about thinking outside the box, or as my clients have called it, "thinking outside the industry." It's probably the most important thing to do because it will lay the foundation for everything else in these pages.

Since I'm not an actor and I don't follow the usual "rules," I have a fresh perspective that lets me see why certain things aren't working, and that gives me the opportunity to propose new solutions.

So let's talk about how most actors think, and how you can start thinking differently.

How Actors at Different Ages Think

I've spoken to thousands of actors during my time as a filmmaker and headshot photographer, and I've interviewed many more since working as a marketing coach.

From speaking to so many people, I've begun to notice a specific pattern in the way most actors speak about their careers and goals. Take a look at this timeline with direct quotes from actors as young as 15 all the way up to age 55:

- **15 Years Old:** *"I want to be on Broadway in lots of shows, and be able to perform in films that play around the world!"*

- **20 Years Old:** *"I would like to get a movie or two under my belt and have that be something that skyrockets me to a successful acting career when I'm older."*

- **25 Years Old:** *"The ultimate dream is to be a professional who can write her own stuff, perform in anything she wants to perform in, and jump in between mediums."*

- **30 Years Old:** *"I don't think being known is a sign of making it - it's a false desire in many ways. If I can be a working SAG actor who has health insurance from SAG, that's all I want."*

- **35 Years Old:** *"I have no desire to be A-list. That's not top of the line successful to me. Being able to create my own art and not have it neutered... that's the goal."*

- **40 Years Old:** *"I want to be able to pay off my student loans with my acting. I want to be able to sustain myself."*

- **45 Years Old:** *"I don't act for the money. I'm not trying to be famous. Lots of people want to be actors so they can be famous and I get that. But I do it because I love playing with other people on stage and being free and spontaneous. It's not at all for the money."*

- **50 Years Old:** *"My dream career would be indie films, feature films, television, Broadway, Off-Broadway, Shakespeare, Musicals; I kinda want to do it all. But there's always somebody who has a better face, nicer hair, bluer eyes, is taller, shorter, or younger/older - something that's never in my control. I can take care of my talent, work, and prep, but there's certain things that will almost always give other people an edge over me."*

- **55 Years Old:** *"In an ideal world, I would be working as one of the best character actors out there. But I just think I'm too lazy for that. You need to eat, sleep, and sh** this job for that to happen."*

Do you notice the pattern I see? Take a look:

- **Young actors from 15 to 25** are unafraid to tell me their dreams of one day creating a career where they are performing on Broadway, acting in major films, and receiving the recognition and rewards they deserve.

- **As actors get into their 30s and 40s**, they pull back on their dreams and tell me that they just want to be a working actor, someone who can afford a modest lifestyle but continue doing work they love. And if I ask them about major goals, they say it would be nice but it's absolutely not why they're doing this.

- **Once actors reach their 50s and beyond**, they're once again unafraid to tell me about their dreams of having amazing opportunities to act in big films and on Broadway, but they seem almost fully set on the idea that it will never happen.

As you can probably guess, the extreme amount of rejection coupled with the confusion of not having a clear, step by step path to follow causes actors to go from "Childlike Dreamer" to "Realistic Adult" to "It'd Be Nice But It's Impossible."

Now of course these are just general trends and don't apply to every actor out there, but I think it's important to see how most actors think. Do you see yourself somewhere on that spectrum?

Some actors truly act just for the enjoyment and they have no big goals. Others keep their dreams of performing in well-known films or in Broadway shows at the forefront of their minds, regardless of their age.

But no matter how you think about it, one thing can probably be agreed upon by everyone:

To have the best chance of achieving your goals, you need to be clear on what they are, keep them at the forefront of your mind, and keep believing they're possible.

If you don't know what your goals are, you'll never achieve much. If you don't keep focused on them, you'll quickly veer off course. And if you start thinking a goal is impossible to achieve, you'll lose all motivation to put effort into achieving it - a phenomenon called "learned helplessness."

Therefore, if you really want to get the most out of this book, I urge you to start by taking your thinking up a notch: First, what do you believe is possible? Now what would be the next level up from there?

If you'd love to work on Broadway one day, what's the next level up? A lead role on Broadway? Winning a Tony Award?

If you want to land a recurring role in a television show one day, what's the next level up? Becoming a series regular? Winning an Emmy?

Don't cut your dreams down just because you think you shouldn't want big things for yourself. If you do that, there truly is no hope left. Remember: no one will ever fight for the dreams you have except you. So don't give them up!

Why So Many Actors Get Stuck

Some actors sit around and wait for opportunities to be handed to them from their agents, managers, or by being discovered in a showcase. Others work hard day in and day out, auditioning and hoping to slowly book bigger and bigger roles over time (but doing relatively the same thing over and over again).

Still others do everything they can each day and get so inundated with work, ideas, and possibilities that they get burned out or too overwhelmed to accomplish anything.

If you're in the first group (the ones that sit around waiting), you probably aren't reading this book. If you're in the second, you're probably feeling frustrated that you've spent years of your life training, building your resume, and making connections, yet you're still being called in for the same small roles over and over again. Even though you're asking your agent or manager to submit you for bigger roles, it feels like casting directors just won't bring you in for them.

And if you're in that third group, you have what's called *Shiny Object Syndrome* - and it's the exact issue that kept me stuck in my business for years. It's telling yourself, "Oh, if I just had *that*, everything would change." And then once you get *that*, nothing changes, so you suddenly realize you actually need something else.

We've all been there at some point. Take a look at the following quotes:

- *"I need a new, more expensive and better headshot."*
- *"I need a professional demo reel (or I need to update my reel)."*
- *"I really need to put myself out there more on social media."*
- *"If I just knew what casting directors wanted, I could give it to them. But how am I supposed to give them what they want if they won't tell me what they're looking for?"*
- *"I need to work on my technique to start booking those higher-level roles."*
- *"I really need to join the union."*
- *"I gotta get an agent (or I need to find a new one)."*
- *"I wish I had more experience and better credits on my resume."*
- *"I need more motivation and energy to deal with the rejection. I need someone to support me and keep me going."*
- *"I need to get better at following up with people."*

I could go on and on, but the truth is, anyone who has those thoughts is most likely focused on fixing a symptom instead of the underlying cause. They're looking at *tactics* instead of *strategy*.

- **Tactic:** A "to do" or "idea" that we think will help us move forward or reach a goal.

- **Strategy:** A high-level plan that organizes a series of tactics in a specific way to achieve an end goal.

Think of a tactic as an ingredient, and a strategy as a recipe designed to make a great meal. You don't want to bake a cake by putting a pile of chocolate, flour, and egg onto a baking sheet and sliding it into the oven, right?

If you go around thinking things like, "I need to update my reel," without first asking whether you're ready for it and if it's the actual best move, you're focused on tactics. You're exhibiting symptoms of Shiny Object Syndrome, and you're bound to stay stuck.

Most people won't talk about Strategy because it's not fun or exciting. Strategy is about thinking, and thinking is boring. It feels like you're not actually accomplishing anything!

It's way more interesting to learn about "The Number 1 Way to Land an Agent," or "The Top 5 Ways Actors Can Use Instagram to Connect with Casting Directors."

But that doesn't work. If you want true success, you need to step back from the tactics. It's time to get out of the metaphorical corn maze you're trapped in. I'm going to help you cut down some of those corn stalks, tie them together, and build a really tall ladder for yourself so you can climb it and look down at the maze from above. Only then will you be able to figure out *where you are* and how to get to *where you want to be*.

Success is not about great ideas or sudden moments of inspiration. It's not about getting lucky or waiting for an opportunity to be handed to you. It's about stepping back for a bit, thinking hard, coming up with a clear strategy, and then implementing it slowly and methodically over the course of years, iterating as you go. Boring, I know, but extremely effective.

This is why I urge you to not jump ahead. Read the book in full. Knowing how to make a great actor website for free is going to be a complete waste of your time if you're not ready for it. Shooting a highly professional headshot is not going not help you if you're constantly sending it out to auditions you're not suited for. And knowing how to find an agent quickly and easily will not help if you sign with the wrong one.

I personally built up my own headshot business from zero to over 150 clients a month with a crappy, unprofessional website and no social media presence. Why? Because I strategized. One of my clients booked a role on Broadway without an Instagram following and a website that was just as basic as mine. Why? Because he strategized.

So what does it really take to get booked on Broadway or land recurring roles on television? Well, there are only six steps, and here they are:

1. **First, you'll reshape the way you think.** Without a complete mindset shift, you're going to have a hard time breaking out of your cycle and booking bigger and better roles.

2. **Next, you'll find your U.S.P.** U.S.P. stands for unique selling proposition, or in other words the qualities that make you different and/or better than other actors out there. Knowing who you are at your core and what you bring to the table makes it infinitely easier to start booking consistent work.

3. **Third, you'll set specific goals and start strategizing.** Here, you'll hyper-target your focus to exactly what you want and set yourself up for success. There's no point wasting your time and energy applying to roles (and memorizing scripts) you aren't right for. We'll also focus on money here because being financially secure will make focusing on your acting work much easier.

4. **Fourth, you'll create (or update) your basic marketing materials.** I call these "basic" because they are the most simple things you'll need to be able to market yourself. Even brand new actors starting out need them: A great headshot and a professionally formatted resume, plus some simple footage of yourself

on camera. Without them you won't be called in for much of anything.

5. **Fifth, you'll start connecting with people and submitting to auditions.** Networking with successful actors, agents, managers, casting directors, filmmakers, and even teachers & professors is crucial if you want to position yourself for success. At this point, you'll actually start submitting and auditioning for the roles you want to start building your resume.

6. **Finally, you'll create your advanced marketing materials and start moving up.** A high-quality demo reel and a clean and professional website are important to cement people's perception of you as a seasoned, professional actor. Once these are created, you'll start strategizing to determine where you want to go next, including getting an agent and/or manager and focusing on booking larger roles.

Most people are surprised when they see the order of these steps. Why am I recommending that you get your headshots so late in the game? And why shouldn't you get a reel together until the last step of the process? Well, it might sound out-of-the-industry and a bit weird, but that's why it's effective.

Thinking and strategizing should always come before taking action steps and investing time or money.

So as you read through this book, you'll see that it's broken into seven parts, with the first six corresponding to the steps outlined above. You'll start by shifting your mindset, you'll then find your brand and strategize on what you really want. Finally, you'll move into putting your marketing materials together , networking, and submitting to projects. Part seven will help you stand out even more by showing you how to be the best you can possibly be.

And don't worry - if you're a seasoned actor thinking that some of this sounds a bit too basic for you, I assure you you'll find tons of value in this book. Things as simple as "finding your brand" will take on a whole new meaning as you read.

So let's jump right in!

You Are Not an Artist

When actors they hear me say that, many are repelled:

"I became an actor because I love art and I want to express myself! How can you tell me I'm not an artist?"

Well, if you want a successful acting career, this is probably one of the most important things to grasp.

You should stop thinking of yourself as an artist and start thinking of yourself as a service provider:

- **An artist** is someone who creates their own work and people come to see it. They usually have a large following of people that want to see them perform or create something simply because *they* created or performed in it.

- **A service provider**, on the other hand, is someone who provides value to others in the form of a service - either by taking photos, designing a website, or you guessed it, acting a role in a film, show, or stage play.

Until the day comes when you have audiences lining up to see a production because *you're* in it, you should think of yourself as a service provider.

Or until the day comes when you're producing your own films or shows (putting your own money on the line), you should think of yourself as a service provider.

As a service provider, you need to focus of just TWO key things:

- **Marketing**, or getting more and more people to know you and want to pay you.

- **Innovation**, or consistently working to become a better actor who provides more and more value to others.

Peter Drucker, a well-known business expert, said that all businesses need to focus on if they want to be highly successful are those two primary things, marketing and innovation. So if what you're spending time on isn't contributing to either, stop.

Most actors just focus on innovation, or wanting to be highly trained. But did you notice that the word Marketing came first? That's because it's even MORE important than innovation if you want success.

How many actors are out there that are absolutely amazing, yet they constantly struggle to find jobs? And how many actors can you think of are terrible, yet you see them every week on TV?

So for the time being, stop thinking of yourself as an *artist* and start looking at yourself as a *service provider*. And stop focusing purely on your Innovation or training, and start focusing on your Marketing. It's gotta be at least a 50/50 split from now on.

If you do that, the day will come (sooner than you think), where people are lining up to see you perform, and you'll finally be recognized as the artist you are at heart.

Serve For Free Before You Charge

If you're just starting, it's extremely important to get some experience on set and start building your resume. Without any experience or connections, you'll find it almost impossible to get paid as an actor unless you're extremely lucky (and I don't recommend counting on luck).

In order to break into any new industry as a service provider, you always have to do some work for free. You must provide value to others before you can expect them to provide value back to you.

I typically recommend acting in at least 3-5 unpaid acting projects that feature you in the forefront for at least one scene before attempting to start booking paid gigs. At bare minimum, you'll gain experience and learn what working on a set is like, and at best you might make some great connections or get strong footage for your reel.

You'll also get an idea of how other people see you (your *type*) so you learn what kinds of roles you should be applying for (more on this later).

Working for free even applied to me as a headshot photographer: When I first started shooting headshots, I had to shoot about five to ten people for free just to build my portfolio because no one was going to pay me for headshots if they couldn't see the work I'd done.

"Okay," you say, "But how do I find these unpaid jobs?"

Try visiting websites like www.castingnetworks.com, www.mandy.com, www.actorsaccess.com, and some other online casting sites. You can also Google "casting calls" and find tons of opportunities for unpaid projects. Just make sure they are in your city and you're able to make it to the auditions. For a detailed listing of some great sites to find casting calls, visit www.martinbentsen.com/get-cast.

Fortunately, unpaid jobs are generally easier to land than paid jobs. When you start out, it should only take a couple months to act in a number of unpaid projects. Think of this time as practicing and experimenting to see if you really want to be in this industry, and what kinds of characters people can see you playing (and you enjoy playing).

The only downside is that the production value of unpaid jobs is often low, meaning they usually don't look very professional. Sometimes it can take a year or more to get footage for a reel because of delays in post-production and directors not wanting to send out screeners before their film has played in a festival.

For this reason, when acting in student films and other unpaid projects for the experience and free footage, be sure to follow up every few months with the director or producer to make sure you get your scenes. A lot of directors forget to give out the footage to actors because they have so many other things going on.

Visit www.martinbentsen.com/get-cast to learn of a great resource I recommend to help with remembering to follow up. I also include some template emails you can use to increase the odds of the director sending you your footage.

Part 2: Find Your U.S.P.

Here's a scenario for you:

Imagine you're at a corner store, standing in front of the refrigerator section with all the drinks. You're trying to decide between two different bottles of water.

One bottle is $0.99 and the other is $2.99.

Besides the price and company name, there is nothing else different about the bottles.

You'd probably buy the $0.99 bottle, right?

Now imagine the same scenario, and both bottles are the same price. Would it be a coin toss for you? It would for me.

Finally, imagine that the $0.99 bottle is just regular water. But the $2.99 bottle has a label telling you that it's been infused with special electrolytes to give you more energy.

Is the $2.99 bottle looking more appealing now?

That's differentiation. That's U.S.P. or Unique Selling Proposition. That's how you'll stand out as an actor.

So the question becomes: Why should a casting director hire you instead of the actor who walked in before you?

You're both talented, highly-trained, friendly, and professional. You both look similar. When it comes down to it, you both seem exactly the same on the surface.

So why would they hire you instead of the other actor?

Well, no reason. It's just a coin toss!

Unless you create a reason.

Specificity is the Name of the Game

"He who trims himself to suit everyone will soon whittle himself away." - Raymond Hull

Have you ever heard the phrase "Jack of all trades, master of none?"

Well, if you want to stay stuck, become a jack of all trades. But if you want success, focus on one extremely specific thing, become a master at it, and the rewards will follow.

Finding your type and brand is the perfect way to become a master at one specific thing - one type of acting and one kind of character.

But wait! Many actors worry about being "typecast" or "pigeonholed." So what then?

Well, remember - you're supposed to think of yourself as a *service provider*, not an *artist*. And worrying about "pigeonholing" is the *artist* in your speaking.

If you're looking at yourself as a service provider, you should feel morally obligated to focus only on the roles you're best at and most enjoy, because you'll do a better job at them and essentially provide your clients (the director and the audience) a better service.

And just in case you're worried, finding a brand does *not* necessarily mean you're pigeonholing yourself. It just means you'll know what types of characters you can play best and you'll focus mostly on those for the next 5-10 years, until your look changes and it becomes time to re-evaluate.

In the long run, actors who find their brand or get "typecast" usually book jobs way more easily because their name starts floating around the industry. Casting directors want them in their projects because of the name recognition and because they know they will be the best at that specific kind of role.

Another important thing to remember is that casting directors find it much easier to remember an actor who is very specific. They'll be much more likely to think of you when the right role pops up, whereas if you're too generalized nothing will ever remind people of you!

The fastest and best way to find the role of your dreams is to get hyper focused on the one character type you play best. Only after you find a brand and you're getting called in all the time (and money is flowing), should you attempt to try new roles if you want to.

"But Martin, wait. I have a question! What if my type is SO specific that I can't find enough opportunities to act?"

That's again the *artist* in your speaking, not the *service provider*. There are so many niches in the world that the opportunities to be successful in any one of them are almost limitless. The more specific you are, the less competition you'll have for roles, so the easier you'll book the jobs that are available. If you're not very specific, you'll apply to lots more roles, but you'll have a much harder time booking them.

Would you rather spend hundreds of hours auditioning for hundreds of roles and booking very few of them, or spend only a few hours auditioning for just a few perfect roles and booking most of them?

Discovering Your Brand & Type

Note: If you're an experienced actor and think you're clear on your brand and type, do NOT skip this chapter. Almost every time I talk to a seasoned actor, I realize a piece of their brand is missing. Please read through this section and do the exercises to get even clearer on your brand even if you think you already have one.

These days, so many actors talk about brand and type, but not many know what the words actually mean!

Here's the simple answer: Your *brand* is essentially your essence; it's a combination of what people see you as physically (which is your *type*) and your deepest personality traits.

Once you define your brand, you'll become more memorable in the industry as an expert at a particular character type, and you'll start to get booked for more and more jobs. As you get busier, you'll start increasing your day rate, and then one day when you have a large enough fan base, you'll be able to break out of your brand and try something completely new if you want.

To understand the importance of brand, I'd like you to imagine two scenarios:

Scenario 1: Not Having a Clear Brand

You are sitting in an audition room, ready to go in and read for a part. You've memorized the lines and think you fit the bill.

You're hoping that they like your look, but you're worried someone else waiting in the room looks more like the character than you. You also don't have that many professional credits under your belt.

They call you in, you do your audition, and then you leave, never to hear from them again. You're a bit annoyed that you wasted your time going out for an audition that never materialized into anything.

Scenario 2: Having a Clear Brand

You are sitting in an audition room, ready to go in and read for a part you specifically chose because it was completely meant for you. It was easy to memorize the lines because you live and breathe the character, and you know you naturally fit the bill.

You know they'll love your look and no one else in the room matches this character type as perfectly as you do. You don't have too many professional credits under your belt, but you're not concerned because your resume is filled with roles that are very similar to the character type you're about to audition for.

They call you in, you have a great time playing a character you absolutely love, and they offer you the job right there on the spot. Booked it, and you know you'll do your best work on set and make amazing new connections with people in the industry.

Which scenario would you rather be in?

If your headshot and marketing materials are bland and don't say anything specific, you'll constantly wonder why you struggle to book jobs. But when you discover your own unique brand, everything changes.

A Short Story on Branding

Check out this story to help illustrate my point:

A client of mine was working as a professional actor for over fifteen years. He had a long list of credits but felt stuck because he was always being offered the same, 1-2 line roles in film, TV, and theater.

At the time, however, he believed he had a clear grasp on his brand because he was often being called in for police officer and detective roles. He told me an acting coach helped define his brand as *strong, burly detective.*

In his old headshot, he looked intense and tried to command a strong, law enforcement look. But the problem was that it wasn't resonating with casting directors.

Whenever he had an audition, he'd do his best to figure out what he thought they wanted, and then he did as much preparation as possible (memorizing everything so he'd be off-book, creating an entire world for the character, and much more).

But after each audition, he heard the same, disheartening words: "Thanks. We'll let you know."

I took him through a series of very specific questions, and after about thirty minutes we came up with this:

A strong, compassionate, and proud detective who can be conceited at times.

This got him excited. He was intrigued by the idea of having a brand that could include words he was proud of while at the same time showing a dark side to make his character more interesting.

I then told him that his *Pride Words* were:

Strength, compassion, and pride.

And that's when everything changed.

His face lit up. I could sense the complete change in his voice as he said those words aloud. He literally became his brand.

Well, the results of that branding session were nothing short of astounding.

Suddenly, he was much clearer on everything, and the nervousness he always felt before auditions evaporated COMPLETELY.

He finally had a brand he was truly proud of, and within less than a month, he was offered his first role on Broadway (something he'd been trying to get for over fifteen years).

He was also offered a guest-star role in an HBO show two weeks later. And one week after that, he was offered representation by a well-known film & television agent in New York (a goal he'd been working towards without success for over three years).

He told me that getting clear on his brand was what made the biggest, immediate difference in his acting career.

How to Find Your Brand

So how do you do go about actually finding your brand? It's simple and easy. Here are the steps:

- **Step 1:** Think of television shows, theater productions, or films you know. Come up with two specific characters from those shows that you could really see yourself playing and write their first names down.

- **Step 2:** With those two names on hand, write down 3-5 words that describe what personality traits they have in common. Put the positive words in a "positive" column and the negative words in a "negative" column.

- **Step 3:** Think of someone who you deeply admire and look up to (ideally you should know them personally). Write down the 3 personality traits they have that you admire most about them in the "positive" column.

- **Step 4:** Next, think of someone you really dislike. Think of the 3 personality traits they have that you most dislike. Write them down in the "negative" column.

- **Step 5- NEGATIVE TRAIT:** Now, take a look at all the words you wrote in the "negative" column. When thinking about those words, which one describes you accurately when you're at your worst? Narrow it down to the one word that most represents you.

- **Step 6 - 3 POSITIVE TRAITS:** Now, take a look at all the positive words you wrote down. Narrow them to the top 3 words that accurately describe you as a person, and the ones you are most proud of. Force yourself to come up with just 3, even if you want to have 4!

- **Step 7 - TYPE:** Now, thinking about the character types you most typically get called in for, what would they be?

Examples are *police officer, student, teacher, intern, gang member, grandmother*, etc. If you don't have enough auditions under your belt to have an answer for this, reach out to at least five people you know and ask them what types of characters they could see you playing. Whatever words come up the most are what you should start with.

- **Step 7:** Now, you'll need to combine the words together into a sentence like so: *A 3 POSITIVE TRAITS TYPE who can be NEGATIVE TRAIT at times*. An example could be *A humble, funny, and daring high school teacher who can be selfish at times*.

Don't take the simplicity of this process lightly. The simple act of coming up with a brand using this process has helped many of my clients immediately start booking more work.

Note: Your brand doesn't need to be perfect yet. You'll be able to refine it over the course of the coming weeks as you read the rest of this book.

Take your brand, write it on a sheet of paper, and tape it to your bathroom mirror (or somewhere you'll see it every day). You'll want to consistently focus on your brand and keep it top of mind so you can refine it and act on it.

Now, something important to be aware of is what I call your *Pride Words.*

Your Pride Words are the three positive words you decided on. These are the words you should be most proud of about yourself and they should be what keep you grounded, especially as you get ready to go in for auditions.

By thinking and focusing on your Pride Words before every audition, you'll notice your nervousness simply melt away, and you'll give performances WAY better than what you have in the past. More on this later in the book.

Using the example from earlier, here is what you'd focus on:

I am humble, funny, and daring.

Keeping focused on your Pride Words (and nothing else) could literally be enough to start getting you booked solid.

But let's go deeper and start strategizing.

Part 3: Get Focused & Strategize

Now that you're clear on your brand and you know what makes you different than other actors out there (your U.S.P. or Unique Selling Proposition), it's time to get focused and start targeting specific projects.

Beyond a brand, you'll need to know the reason why you act, what characters you're most suited for, what shows or films you'll want to focus on, and why you want to achieve your goals.

Without getting focused and coming up with an overall direction for where you're headed, it's easy to lose track of what you really want and get stuck.

Find Your Purpose & Get Hyper Focused

Those who succeed are those who give themselves a chance and are willing to take risks.

And those who give themselves a chance and are willing to take risks are those who have something to fight for.

So why are you doing this? What are you fighting for? What's the deep-rooted reason you're an actor?

By finding the answer to this question, you'll be unconsciously pulled towards making your goals become real, and it will seem almost effortless.

Discover and Clarify Your Acting Purpose

First, a quick question: Have you ever heard that we only use 10% of our brains?

Do you really believe that?

Most people say no, because science and evolutionary theory has said that whatever you don't use, you lose (in order to preserve energy). So based on that, science has proven that in fact we do use 100% of our brains.

But here's the interesting part: That 10% people talk about is actually partially true. It's called the conscious part of our brains - the part where we do our thinking and regular day to day processing of information. It's basically where we live.

But the other 90% of our brain is actually subconscious, which means we're not aware of it. The subconscious is the part that controls our emotions, the beating of our hearts, and even the things we like and don't like to do.

Example: Do you like eating tomatoes? Well, you don't choose to like tomatoes consciously, it's your subconscious that determines whether you'll like them or not.

So then the question becomes: What if you could tap into that other 90% of your brain and start using it to propel your acting career forward?

Almost all successful people are successful because the subconscious part of their mind drives them towards doing what's necessary to reach their goals. If you could somehow reprogram your subconscious mind and tap into that remaining 90%, you'd automatically have 9X increased drive, excitement, and focus, with much less anxiety and stress.

Negative emotions generally cause us to avoid taking the actions required to reach the peak places in life, so if there were a way to avoid those emotions, we'd be so much more effective.

I believe that we each have a purpose to fulfill in our life. We each have something to contribute to this world, and until we find it, we can never access that other 90% of our brains.

I also believe that you've decided to be an actor for a reason, but a reason you might not even be fully conscious of yet. If you can find out what that reason is and tap into its power, that's when real success will come.

How I Found My Own Life Purpose

For a while I was absolutely obsessed with Asian martial arts films. Donnie Yen was my hero. One day, while scanning through Netflix, I happened to come across a Chinese television series called *The Legend of Bruce Lee*.

The first episode starts and guess what I find out? Bruce Lee was a cha-cha dancer before he did kung fu! He was just like me, in the sense that he had no real idea of what he wanted to do in his life. He wasn't from a wealthy family and had no connections, but suddenly he got really interested in kung fu because of a fight he was in with some bullies at his school.

He then became obsessed with everything about kung fu, and after a number of years of studying it he eventually found himself in the United States. It was then that he learned that no one in the U.S. had ever heard of kung fu or had any idea that China was the original inventor of martial arts. He suddenly became obsessed with showing the world that China deserved more respect and should not be called the "Sick Man of East Asia," as people used to say.

As Bruce became obsessed with the idea of bringing respect back to China, he started to realize that that was his true life purpose and the only thing he really cared about. He took crazy risks and continuously put himself on the line for what he believed in, because if he didn't achieve his life-goal, what would be the point of even existing?

As I watched the show and saw how incredible his achievements were, and how much he was willing to sacrifice for what he believed in, along with the level of success, fame, and fortune he achieved in the process, I couldn't help but think to myself, "This is all because he found his life purpose, his reason for being."

As I realized that, I began to think about all the other majorly successful people in life... those who've become mega famous, wealthy and/or successful, or those whose names have been remembered throughout time. Abraham Lincoln, George Washington, Rosa Parks, Helen Keller, Mother Theresa, Nelson Mandela, Jesus Christ, and many, many others.

What do they all have in common? Well, whether you like them or hate them, it's clear that they all found a life purpose they believed so strongly in that they sacrificed years of their lives and moved mountains to make it a happen. Not only did they believe it was possible, but they believed they were the ones meant to achieve it, and that in the end, it would absolutely be worth the sacrifice.

After I realized this, I couldn't sleep at all that night. Why? Because I had no idea what my own life purpose was.

But I knew at least one thing: the only way for me to reach the biggest goals in my life would be to discover my own life purpose and then work to achieve it.

So What Did I Discover?

At first I started thinking about what I really loved to do. As it turns out, I had already built a fairly successful business called City Headshots (www.cityheadshots.com) because I really loved photography and video work. But as I thought more, I realized I might not be 100% passionate about photography alone.

The photographers I hired for my team were passionate, but I was personally even more interested in the psychology behind why people were often uncomfortable on-camera, and why it could be hard to get clients to relax at times.

I remember how as I grew my business, I would get angry, freaked out, or overwhelmed at times. At one point I got so sick of my emotional overreactions that I decided to try to create a tool that would allow me to coach myself. After a few months of work, I had developed a set of questions that actually allowed me to explore my own unconscious mind. Basically the tool could lead me to uncover why I felt a certain way about things, and why feeling that way actually made no sense - this way I could easily change it.

Since I had already created this tool to help uncover my unconscious thoughts, I asked, "Why not create a similar tool that could help me find my life purpose?

And it was then that I thought, "Maybe my life purpose is to help other people find theirs?"

This got me excited. I explored the idea more and played around with it for a few months, and eventually learned that what I was most passionate about was helping people reach their goals. And I absolutely loved working with actors.

So here is the set of questions I developed to help actors find out why they do what they do at the deepest level.

Just fill in your answers to each question and by the end of this 10 minute process, you'll have a pretty good idea of what's most important to you in your acting career.

1. On the surface, what do you think is most important to you when it comes to acting?

2. What kind of roles or characters would you play if you didn't have to worry about money? What type of acting work would you do? Feel free to think about the brand

you discovered earlier and work that into your answer if you'd like.

3. What big goal would you try to achieve in your acting career if no matter what you did, you couldn't fail?

4. Look at what you wrote for questions 2 and 3. How can you combine those answers together into one primary goal or focus?

5. Now, how can you ensure that you're helping others in this process?

6. How can you ensure that you're constantly growing, learning, and improving as a person in this process?

7. Who would you be known as in the world?

8. Simplify that down to a single statement: The reason I act is because _____.

Now that you have a clear acting purpose, you should be feeling excited. This should feel like something you're truly passionate about and want to take action on!

If it doesn't, go back and modify your answers until it does, and then you can move onto the next section.

Figure Out the Roles That Suit You

Now that you know your acting purpose, it's time to break it down into smaller chunks. If you're worried that your acting purpose is different than what you're currently doing, that's totally fine. At least you know what it is now so you can start moving towards on it!

So how do you use your acting purpose and newfound brand to figure out the three primary types of roles you will focus on?

Let's use an example acting purpose to create some sample answers. Let's pretend your purpose is to *win an academy award while playing dark characters in such a way that the audience feels deep empathy for them.* And let's say your brand is *the strong, driven, and passionate father who can be violent at times.*

How can you break those down into three specific roles?

- **Role 1:** Play fathers who are members of gangs.

- **Role 2:** Play fathers who are emotionally distraught and calling out for help.

- **Role 3:** Play financially successful fathers who have no connection to their families and wish they did.

These are just three random ideas, and yours will probably be completely different.

So what are the three different roles you can see yourself playing? Come up with them now.

Next, think of theater productions, TV shows, or films that are casting now or will be in the near future (check out www.martinbentsen.com/get-cast for some up to date casting resources that will have this information readily available). Come up with at least 10 specific shows or films you could see yourself acting in within one of the three roles you came up with.

Write down the 10 show or film names and keep them in a safe place because we'll be referencing them later in this book.

Why Do You Want This So Bad?

Most of the time, *how* you're going to do something is far less important than *why* you want to do it. The reason for this is because without a strong enough *why* you'll never find the *how* (or be willing to do the work required) and you'll give up.

I could hand you a detailed, step by step plan on how to get the athletic body of your dreams, but would you really be willing to put in the effort required if you didn't have much of a reason to want to get fit?

On the other hand, if I withheld the step by step instruction plan but you wanted to get into great shape so badly because of how healthy you'd be, who you'd impress, and how awesome you'd feel, do you think you'd put in the effort to go find information, tools, or someone else who could help you? Much more likely.

The same is true for any goal you have. If you have enough reasons why you want something, chances are you'll be motivated enough to go out and make it happen.

So your next step is to figure out why you want to get booked in these 10 shows or films so badly.

1. First, come up with a list of 10 reasons why life will be so amazing if you land these dream roles. Think of where you'll be 10 years from now if you booked them all and everything came to fruition!

2. Second, come up with a list of 10 reasons why you'd be extremely sad and unhappy if you looked back on your life 10 years from now and felt regret that you never made it happen.

Keep these reasons handy and refer back to them any time you start to slow down, feel overwhelmed, or get tired. These reasons are your fuel!

Write a Compelling Biography

Now that you've found your Acting Purpose and you're clear on your brand, it's time to write a compelling biography that makes you proud. This bio needs to be so emotionally charged that whenever you read it, you'll suddenly feel a charge of excitement inside you - a fire should light up and move you to action.

Most actor bios, however, are old-fashioned and boring! There's no emotional energy and the actor who wrote it doesn't even want to read it himself! If you don't want to read your own bio, who else will?

Here's what most actor bios look like (although many are much longer and look like one humungous, overwhelming paragraph):

John Smith has appeared in numerous film, television, and theatre productions. You may have seen him in The Matrix, Titanic, Jurassic Park and E.T., to name just a few. John's ability to work as a fight choreographer has been recognized by the University of Awesome Actors with the Best Fight Choreographer award. John studied acting at Master Acting School, graduating with a MFA in 2008. A native of Southern California, John now lives in New York City and can be reached online through his website at www.iamjohnsmith.com.

Even if your credits are as good as John's, casting directors won't care that they're in your bio - they'll find your credits when they look at your resume.

Besides his parents, the only other person who might take the time to fully read a bio like that would be John's grandma or his agent or manager - but would you want them to have to slog through all that? An agent or manager will probably just interview you instead to find out what they need to know.

So here is a simple checklist you can use to determine whether your bio needs some work:

- It must be emotionally charged and show the excitement and passion you have for acting. This is key.

- Keep it short and easily skimmable - break it up into 2-3 short paragraphs.

- You can write it in first person, but be humble about your achievements.

- Ensure you list your most important achievements right away.

- Explain in at least 1-2 sentences why you do what you do.

- Mention at least 1-2 special skills towards the end of your bio.

- If you want, feel free to make your bio funny or include any quirks you have so it's more interesting to read.

Here is a template for how your bio can be written:

- **Paragraph 1:** Who are you, why do you love acting, and what are the three most noteworthy professional accomplishments you've achieved?

- **Paragraph 2:** What types of projects do you most enjoy working on and why? And what is the best thing you bring to every project you work on?

- **Paragraph 3:** Mention any special skills and quirks you have, and then include your long-term goal.

Here is a sample bio, written in the above format (whilst keeping the checklist in mind as well):

My name is John Smith and I freaking love acting. I've had the amazing opportunity to appear in a number of major films including The Matrix, Jurassic Park, and E.T., and I've also been fortunate to have performed alongside Leonardo DiCaprio in Titanic.

Getting deep into character to play dark, brooding roles is where I excel, and I have the most fun playing detective types, which might be related to my father's work as a law enforcement officer. Something I pride myself in bringing to every set is a highly professional demeanor and a willingness to go above and beyond to help the cast and crew in any way I can. I truly love acting and would do it every day if I could! Being able to breath life into words on a page is a truly humbling experience.

In addition to acting and singing, I can also fight; I'm highly trained in stunt work and combat training, and I've worked as a fight choreographer for six films. I have a soft spot for yellow M&M's (just kidding), and my long-term goal is to one day perform as lead in a popular Broadway musical.

Now you'll no doubt find information online advising you against writing in first person and saying to keep things ultra-professional, but in my humble opinion, that just comes off as too corporate. Listing your accomplishments one by one is really the job of your resume. With my own clients, I've found that this form of "outside-the-industry" thinking can make a big difference in how memorable you are to casting directors!

Most busy people will only read your bio if they're interested in getting more information than what they could find in your resume, so a bio is the perfect opportunity to get across your personality and connect with them in a more "human" way. The more relatable you seem, the more likely they'll want to meet you!

Revisit your answers from the "Find Your Purpose and Get Hyper-Focused" chapter and use it as a driver to help you create a strong, emotionally-charged bio.

Final Note: After writing your bio, you might consider creating a version that's written in 3rd person just in case you need it (this should take just a minute to do). For your website and marketing materials, you'll use the 1st person bio, but for other uses (such as show/film websites, articles, and/or playbills), the 3rd person version will make more sense.

Make Money a Non-Issue

Now that you've figured out your purpose, you have a strong bio telling your story, and you really know what roles and shows/films you want to target, it's important to do a quick reality check:

Do you have enough money to make this happen? Before we start diving into tactics and working on booking auditions, I want to ensure your finances are secure.

In this section, we'll discuss how to save and earn more money so you're not wondering where your next meal will come from.

Now, take a look at these two quotes:

- *"There's no other job where you're asked to prepare so much - working unpaid - to go in for something that will most likely result in nothing."*

- *"I shouldn't be going out tonight because I could be using that money for my acting career."*

Have you ever felt like that?

Many indie films and small theaters (and even some large ones) don't pay well, and so to make ends meet, most actors are forced into looking for low-paying, flexible jobs.

It's imperative that you position yourself in a financially secure position if you want acting success. The stories you've heard of actors like Sylvester Stallone living out on the street until their big breaks are extremely rare, and for every happy ending there are millions of sad ones that you never hear about.

Because acting requires so much mental focus, worrying about where your next paycheck is coming from will be a distraction that causes your audition technique to suffer. It's a vicious cycle where less money creates more worry, which creates worse performances, which lead to less bookings, which creates even less money, and so on.

So the goal with this section is to get you financially secure so your mind is free to focus 100% on your acting.

The 20/30/50 Rule for Easy Money Management

I'm going to assume you already have some sort of part-time or full-time job that earns you a specific amount of income each month (if you don't, keep reading because we'll talk about earning more soon).

The 20/30/50 rule is an easy way to manage your money so you don't have to worry about not having enough in your accounts.

So how does it work?

It's very simple. First, you need to figure out how much money you make each month on average. Even if it changes, find your baseline income. Let's pretend you have a part-time job that earns about $1,500 a month and you also make at least $300 a month from acting.

This means you bring in $1,800 per month on average.

Now, take that $1,800 and subtract your monthly required living expenses. Let's say you have $700 rent each month, and then another $700 in utilities, food, etc.

If we subtract your monthly costs, $1,800 minus $700 minus $700 equals $400 left over.

Take that $400 and divide it up into percentages, 20%, 30%, and 50%.

- 20% goes towards savings. ($80)

- 30% goes towards fun money. ($120)

- 50% goes towards your career. ($200)

Take this money and put it into separate accounts or sub-accounts (or just keep track of the totals) so you know how much you can spend. Try not to spend it each month unless you absolutely have to - the goal is that you save it up over time eventually have plenty of money laying around for when you need it.

If you strictly follow this for a year or two, not only will you have plenty of money to further your career, have fun, and have a safety net for slower times, but you'll also have built a savings mentality that will help you greatly in the long run!

Don't Waste Your Hard-Earned Money

Did you know? As of 2017:

- Just 41% of actors were employed during pilot season and 87% of actors were typically unemployed at any given point in the year.

- The median annual earnings for a union actor was just $8,448.00 per year.

- A yearly income of at least $50,000 a year was recommended to be financially stable in NY or LA.

You definitely DON'T want to lose your hard-earned money in this expensive industry. Below, I've compiled a list of the top five ways actors can save up to $3,450 per year!

1: Submissions & Prints - Save up to $150

How often do you order 8x10 prints of your headshots? And when you order them, how many do you get? Most actors will say, "Once every year or two, and 100 copies."

And how often do you need to hand in hard-copy prints at an audition these days? Rarely. Most submissions are done digitally now, so you won't need many hard copies.

The industry has consistently made it sound like you should be ordering hundreds of copies of your headshot and mailing them out to all the casting directors and agents in your city. The truth is, none of that is needed anymore, and unsolicited mailings often get thrown straight in the trash without even being opened.

If you do the math, and even if we assumed that you needed to hand in a hard-copy headshot at every audition (usually you don't), you'd still need to go on an audition consistently once every six days to use up 100 headshots before you're ready to update your headshot two years later.

Again, that's assuming you hand in a hard copy headshot at EVERY audition. In reality, you might only need one for every 5 auditions because of digital submissions these days, which would mean you'll need to go on an audition almost DAILY to use them all up before your next photoshoot.

What to do instead: Just buy 25 copies, or maybe 50 at most. You can save about $50 right there and still have plenty of copies to last until your next shoot. And if you run out, just buy a few more. And don't waste $100 mass mailing them out.

Savings total so far? $150

2: Scammers and Liars - Save up to $500

Have you ever experienced the classic actor scam where they say you're the most amazing actor they've ever seen and they want to promote and market you to get you into all kinds of huge projects? For a flat fee of $500? It's so awesome, right?

Yeah, right...

You absolutely MUST avoid those scams! Many actors have had thousands of dollars stolen from them in hopes of their dreams coming true based on lies they've been told.

Scams abound in places like Craigslist, online casting networks, and even on Google. Remember, agencies and managers should NEVER charge you. They should only take a percentage of what you earn after they find you work. If you're unsure about something, ask people you trust in the industry for their opinion.

What to do instead: Real success takes time and effort, so remember that if something sounds too good to be true, it probably is. Avoid scams and do your homework before forking over your money to some weirdos working in a creepy back office.

Savings total so far? $500 + $150 = $650 Total Savings

3: Unhelpful Seminars & Classes - Save up to $300

Do you love honing your craft in classes and auditioning in front of casting directors and agents?

Unfortunately, some of those "opportunities" are actually just marketing ploys to line the pockets of the people running them. Did you know that in some cases, the "casting director" you're auditioning for is actually just an assistant who can't help you, even if they wanted to?

Not to be too negative, but many classes and seminars can be a waste of money. You could easily get the same information for free online. YouTube is a great place to learn something useful instead of having your money swiped by the industry.

Of course, there are definitely many real, valuable classes and acting coaches that organize information in a helpful way and provide you real value, but you need to protect yourself from the fake ones.

If, on average, you spend about $100 each month on classes, and about 25% of those classes are not providing you much value, you can easily save yourself $300 a year.

What to do instead: Do your homework. Look up genuinely valuable classes, research the background of who is running them, and check to see whether the information they teach can be easily found for free online. If everything seems fine, give it a go. But if anything is questionable, stay away.

Savings total so far? $650 + $300 = $950 Total Savings

4: Hiring When You Can Do It for Free

Some actors feel forced into spending $500 or more to have someone professionally design their website.

Unfortunately, most of the money they spend winds up covering the cost of flashy animations that freeze up and make the user experience a nightmare for casting directors, agents, and filmmakers. It's much better to keep your website simple and create it yourself when you're first getting started.

What about paying for self-tapes (audition videos)? Most actors do self-tapes at least ten times per year, so there's a huge savings opportunity there. They've been told that they should only submit highly professional self-tapes for auditions, but the question is, what does the word "self" mean? The title itself should clue you in to the value of hiring someone else to do your self-tape (hint: very little).

Save $50 each time and do it yourself, the way it was intended. Don't be fooled by the clever marketing tactics of those who offer "self-tapes" as a service, unless they're giving you active feedback on your audition and coaching you to make it better.

Most casting directors don't care whether the lighting is perfect in your audition video; they only care if they can see and hear you clearly enough to decide whether they like your acting ability. Only invest in self-tapes if money is not an issue.

Finally, stay away from managers unless they're really good. A great manager should be actively finding you work or helping you manage your extremely busy schedule. Good managers are very selective with who they work with.

Many actors have been told that having a manager means they've "made" it, when in fact in fact there are scammers out there who claim to be "managers" and simply pocket 10% or more of your earnings while providing you very little value.

If a manager doesn't seem selective with who they take on (meaning they immediately say "yes" without putting you through an audition process or in-depth interview), you can save yourself a bundle by avoiding them. This can add up to another $1,000 or more in savings each year.

What to do instead: Design your own website for free using software like www.weebly.com or www.wix.com to save $500. Use your smartphone and a $10 phone tripod to do your own self-tapes to save another $500 per year. You can set up a white piece of cardboard behind you while using window light for a professional look (make sure a rug is on the floor so there is minimal echo). Finally, manage yourself at the beginning of your career - don't pay someone else to meddle in your affairs and charge you unless they are legit. This can save you another $1,000.

Savings total so far? $950 + $2,000 = $2,950 Total Savings

Note - if you teach yourself how to design your own website, you can go and start offering that service to other actors and charging $500 per website!! We'll talk more about earning money on the side in a moment.

5: Not Investing in Good-Quality Headshots

Many new actors believe they can get away with using a cheap headshot or having their friend take their headshot.

After they've spent 3-4 years in the industry wondering why they haven't been getting called in much, they finally decide to bite the bullet and spend $500 or more on a professional headshot, and that's when EVERYTHING changes.

Why does everything change? Because casting directors almost always skip past actors who use unprofessional headshots when they're deciding who to bring in for an audition.

They immediately assume you're not serious about your acting career if you haven't invested real money in a high-end headshot.

Do you think the headshot you're using is fine as it is? Consider comparing it to pro-level headshots (just search google for "professional actor headshots"). Find whichever images look the best and then ask yourself whether your headshot really looks that good.

We'll discuss headshots more soon, but for now, keep in mind that it's painfully obvious to experienced casting directors and agents if you haven't invested in a good headshot. Lighting, makeup, background, and expression are all factors that combine together to create a stand-out image that gets taken seriously.

An unprofessional headshot will probably cost you THOUSANDS of dollars in missed opportunities.

That being said, most actors have been told they need to spend *lots* of money to get a good headshot, and while this is somewhat true, there is definitely a limit to how much they need to spend.

At a certain point, you're only paying for the photographer's name. The technical quality of a $1,500 headshot is often no better than the quality of a $500 shot if your photographer specializes in headshots. The main difference is the photographer's name.

What to do instead: Plan out exactly what you're going to do ahead of time so you can get pro-level headshots even with a no-name photographer and save yourself $500. Figure out your best side to see how light can flatter and complement your facial features, and practice different expressions to see what character types you can play best. Check out the free in-depth guide I've put together for directing yourself by visiting my members-only page at www.martinbentsen.com/get-cast.

Savings total? $2,950 + $500 = $3,450

Act In Commercials for Extra Cash

Acting in commercials is a great way to help pay the bills, especially if you're willing to out in the work required to start booking consistent work.

Here's a story to illustrate this point:

I was friends with a professional actor who got sick of having to choose between doing what he loved and paying his bills, so one day he decided to see what it would be like to try acting in commercials. He just so happened to have the right combination of personality, professionalism, and work ethic, and after about six months what resulted completely changed his life:

He booked a national commercial series and earned 3X what many Americans make in a year from a single job.

Check out the first commercial of the series (The Dodge® Ram Challenge) at www.martinbentsen.com/get-cast.

In his own words:

"I'm driving a convertible right now through the streets of New York. I'm on 125th street. All due to the fact that I did a commercial. A freakin' commercial... You know what I mean?"

My friend earned over $150,000 from the two-week job.

Imagine how it would feel if you knew your bills were taken care of and you had enough money coming in from commercials that you could quit your day job?

Well, don't expect it to happen overnight, but if you put in the effort and follow the advice in this section, that could be your reality sooner than you think. With the extra money, following through on your acting dreams will be much easier.

First, Where Do You Find Commercial Auditions?

If you're in a huge rush to start submitting and don't want to learn strategy, I've compiled a list of the most up to date places you can find reliable commercial casting calls at www.martinbentsen.com/get-cast.

However, I discourage you from submitting if you're not fully prepared - it will be a waste of your time and could even create a bad first impression with casting directors. Instead, read or skim the rest of this article first!

Booking Commercials Requires a Mindset Shift

Commercials sound great on the surface because of all the benefits:

- **Many of them pay well** - commercials can be a quick way to earn money because they're shorter and often pay better than other acting gigs.

- **They can create opportunities for "other" work** - some commercial directors also shoot films and other projects, so keeping in touch with them can create opportunities for your primary acting work down the line.

- **They are looking for anyone and everyone** - gone are the days where commercials only used extremely attractive actors and actresses. Nowadays, companies are looking for all different people, and there are always new commercials casting. This means the opportunities are almost limitless.

- **You can build a commercial resume quickly** - since commercials are often just 1-2 days instead of 1-2 months like films or 6-12 months like theater runs, you can build your commercial resume quickly. That will lead to more and more jobs - kind of like a snowball effect.

- **You can also build a commercial reel quickly** - since commercials are shot and rolled out so fast, you can build a significant reel in a short time frame. No need to wait years until a film is finished to get footage for your reel.

- **You can get some quick wins in your acting career** - if you do it right and start booking, you'll start building confidence in yourself, especially if you've struggled to get work in other areas. You can build up your experience and connections doing commercials and then shift back into film, TV, and theater later on.

With all these benefits, why is it that some actors still struggle to book commercials? And why do others seem to just land more and more jobs?

Well, there's a crucial mindset that successful commercial actors have, and it's related to the idea of "selling."

Most people think that selling is sleazy:

- *"I don't want to be like those used car salesmen!"*

- *"Commercials are not fulfilling to me because I feel slimy."*

Well, if you want any level of success as a commercial actor, you'll need to start by shifting your perspective on sales so you can feel fulfilled doing commercials.

Focus on the fact that the companies you're working for are actually providing a valuable product or service designed to help change people's lives for the better.

By acting in commercials, you're not being salesy or sleazy, you're actually being helpful and providing value to people!

If someone doesn't need or want what the commercial is selling, they just won't buy it. But putting the offer out there is extremely important, otherwise society would never have the opportunity to move forward.

Once you make this mindset shift and start truly enjoying the commercial acting world, there will be a dramatic change in the energy you project in auditions, which will lead you to start booking more of them.

Getting Things Together for Your Commercial Acting Career

Now that you've shifted your mindset around sales and you're ready to dive in, it's important to make sure you get the right training and present yourself properly.

- **Stop submitting to every commercial** - The biggest mistake most actors make around trying to book commercial auditions is that they just submit to every commercial they see without stopping to think, "Is this right for me?" You need to be highly targeted if you want success, meaning you'll have to take some time to figure out what roles are best for you. Think of it as doing 80% of the work up front so everything else is easier.

- **Get improv training** - Take at least 2-3 improv classes if you haven't already. Why? Because most commercial directors are looking for an actor who can add something unique to their production. If you think you're naturally good at improv and don't need classes, just remember that most casting directors won't bring you in unless they see improv training on your resume.

- **Get screen acting training** - In addition to focusing on improv, you also need to make sure your screen acting is up to par. Some actors try to transition into commercials straight from theater without proper training, and the results are painfully obvious to a casting director. Screen acting, whether it be for TV, film, or commercials, is NOT the same as theater, and if you're not fully trained on-screen you'll have a very hard time booking jobs.

- **Position yourself as a commercial actor** - Casting directors are more likely to book you if you look like you specialize in commercials. To do this, ensure all your marketing materials are focused on commercial acting. Shoot a set of commercial headshots with a big, bright, cheery smile. Create a resume specifically for your commercial work. You can also write a bio and create an entire webpage on your site devoted to your commercial work. The more you look like you're a specialist, the more likely commercial casting directors and agents will want to work with you.

- **List your special skills** - Special skills can be an important factor when it comes to deciding on one actor over another. If you can juggle, handstand, toss pizza dough, or do any other out-of-the-ordinary thing, list it on your resume and online casting profiles. Occasionally casting directors will jump onto Actor's Access to search for actors with those skillsets, and who knows, you might just be invited to audition for a pizza commercial! Visit www.martinbentsen.com/get-cast to watch an interview I did with a casting director as she talks about how important special skills are for your resume.

- **Create a great commercial reel** - A commercial reel is extremely helpful for casting directors to decide whether they want to bring you in or not. In less than two minutes, they can see what you've been in and how you look on-camera. Don't create a reel with both commercial and legit work - it's much better to have a reel dedicated solely to commercials. And if you have not been in a commercial yet and have no footage, there are tons of directors shooting spec commercials who need actors. A great spec commercial can instantly push your commercial acting career ahead by a year or more!

Knocking the Commercial Audition Out of the Park:

Once you actually arrive at the audition, there are some things you can do to improve your chances of booking the role:

- **Ask the casting assistant if you have questions** - If you're unsure about something, feel free to ask the casting assistant. They want you to do your best!

- **Do not change what you planned** - Some actors see others sitting in the audition room and start to get worried that the choices they made could be wrong. And they decide to change up everything! Don't let this be you or you can kiss the opportunity goodbye. Stick to your guns, stay focused on your brand, and believe in the initial choices you made!

- **Say your Pride Words in your head right as you walk into the audition** - Think of your Pride Words and connect with them at a deep level, and really feel them. It's almost impossible to feel nervous and confident at the same time, so if you focus on the parts of your brand that you're most proud of and put yourself into that character, your nervousness will evaporate completely.

- **Enter with a genuine smile** - If you're friendly with those in the room, they'll appreciate it and you'll make a good first impression. Don't just walk in and immediately say, "My name is _____ and I'm here to audition for _____," without actually greeting anyone.

- **Be confident in yourself** - Some actors come in and start by apologizing. This is really awkward and makes casting directors uncomfortable. Instead, take pride in yourself and feel confident when you come in. Focus on your brand and remember that you're there not as some lowly, unsuccessful actor, but as a potential partner that will represent their company!

- **Be natural, not theatrical** - This goes along with studying screen acting. Make sure you don't over enunciate words or speak too robotically (or over the top). Talk in a natural manner the same way you would if you were having a conversation with a friend.

- **Do not talk over them** - When the casting director gives you feedback, just be quiet until they're completely finished. Lots of actors will say, "Yeah, yeah..." as they receive notes, and it makes the casting director feel like they're not being heard. Just listen quietly until they're done and if you have a follow-up question, feel free to ask. Then thank them for the feedback in a way that shows them you're excited to try it the new way!

I list plenty more audition tips later on in this book, but for now these should get you booking some commercial auditions.

Do you want to book even more commercials? Check out www.martinbentsen.com/get-cast for a much more in-depth guide.

Start a Side Hustle and Make $500 Extra Each Month

What would it feel like if suddenly you had some extra cash?

And not just $20 or $50. How about $500?

Earning an extra $500 per month from freelancing would be a welcome addition to almost anyone's income, and it's easier than you think to achieve.

Think about what it would be like if you bought yourself a cheap digital SLR camera and learned how to shoot behind the scenes photos for filmmakers. If you could become a set photographer, anyone who hires you as an actor could also become a client, which would give you a lot more money to work on your own projects and build your acting career.

Imagine if you charge $100 per day, and you shoot 3 days each week. Suddenly you have an extra $1,200 per month coming in. Now what if you charged $300 per day? That's still inexpensive and suddenly you have $3,600 per month and you still have four off-days each week - plus you have extra opportunities to network with people on set every day!

Working for yourself is important when you're an actor and it can lead people to perceive you differently. I actually know of an actor who edits films and cuts demo reels. He invested in the program Final Cut and taught himself basic editing skills. He edits about 5-10 reels each month and charges $250 per reel, and makes a clean $2,000 each month editing at night and has fun doing it. Then he has the freedom to do what he loves, which is acting.

So here are the steps to start a side hustle:

Step 1: Figure Out What You Want to Do

The first question to ask yourself is, "What are you good at?"

What do you enjoy doing besides acting that you think people would find value in? Below is a list of ideas you might want to consider because they are popular and people are usually willing to pay for them:

- Writing & Editing
- Transcription of Videos & Audio
- Videography and/or Editing Video
- Graphic Design
- Web Design
- Photography
- Presentation Design (like PowerPoint, etc.)
- Social Media Posting for Companies
- Private Tutoring
- Personal Training
- Life Coaching
- Martial Arts Instruction
- Dance Classes or Choreography
- Acting Classes
- Acting in Commercials (a separate article and strategy)
- Dating & Matchmaking
- Bookkeeping or Tax Filing (if you somehow enjoy this)

- Travel Planning

- Personal or Virtual Assistant

- Personal Chef

- Courier Services

- Pet Services (grooming, walking, training, etc.)

- Home Organizing

- Fashion Stylist

- Makeup Artist

- Child Care & Babysitting

Pick one of the categories above or make one up (note that if you're going to make one up you'll need to ensure people actually want the service by asking around).

Step 2: Figure Out Who You Want to Help

Who is your ideal target customer? What type of person would you enjoy working with? It's important that you select someone who would benefit from the service you offer AND be a pleasure to work with. If you hate working with certain people, you won't do good work and won't get referrals. It's up to you to make sure that you're being yourself.

Let's pretend you decide you want to earn extra cash babysitting because it's not too time consuming and you don't mind kids. Who would you be looking to market to? Ideally women in their mid thirties who have busy lives and want to free up some time. You'll probably want to work with people who are easy to physically get to - people who live close to you - unless you're doing something like website design where you can work with people anywhere in the world.

One other thing to consider that's extremely important is whether the person has the ability to pay you. Don't market your babysitting services to people in their mid twenties because they probably earn less money than someone in their thirties and won't want to pay you.

Pick an ideal client you'd want to work with and decide what types of people you will say NO to.

Step 3: Figure Out Why They Buy What You Sell

When you speak with these people and they are considering working with you, you'll need to know why they buy what you sell. What are they really buying? A common phrase in the business and marketing community is: "Consumers don't buy features, they buy benefits."

Example: In the case of a personal chef, they are not hiring you because they need to eat food. They could *easily just go to a grocery store and make their own meals. They are hiring you because they want more free time, they want to enjoy delicious, home cooked meals, they want the convenience of not having to worry about shopping for groceries, and some people might even want to feel a certain level of importance, or status. The <u>feature</u> of what you sell is delicious, home cooked meals. But the <u>benefits</u> are the free time, amazing taste, convenience, and feelings of importance they will get when they hire you.*

Now in the case of the babysitter, why would they hire you? They are not looking for someone to take care of their child, because they could easily do that. They are looking for more free time to spend with their significant others on dates, they are looking for an easier, more relaxed life, they are looking for someone they can trust completely, and they might even be looking for someone who will engage with their child more than they can because of their busy schedule. So the *features* you're selling are babysitting services, but the *benefits* are free time, an easier & relaxed life, someone they can trust, and help with ensuring their child gets the proper attention he/she needs.

Talking about benefits is more important than features because almost all people buy based on emotion instead of logic.

So what is the main feature you provide? And what are the five biggest benefits the feature (or features) will provide?

Think of emotional benefits and what hiring you will mean to them.

Step 4: Figure Out Your Packages & Pricing

You'll now need to figure out exactly what your clients will get when they hire you. What is the service you're providing them exactly?

For instance, if you're a personal trainer, what tangible benefits can they expect to see within the first week, month, and three months of working with you? If you're a babysitter, how does working with you look? What will you actually do for the client and what is your process like?

Most likely they'll hire you for a certain amount of time - a specific number of hours, and you'll charge a certain amount per hour. They can expect their child to be taken care of, fed, entertained, and be put to bed at certain hours.

What will you charge and what pricing model will you use (hourly fee, monthly retainer, project fee, etc.)? What will your clients receive when they work with you? Keep things simple and easy for the client to understand.

Step 5: Do a Few Free Projects for Clients You Know

Before you can actually start charging people for a service, you need to offer it a few times for free to get some satisfied clients that can either refer you to their friends or write a glowing review for you. The best place to offer free business is to people you already know, but if you don't know anyone who would need your services you can also post a listing to Craigslist.

When you do the service, make sure to do a great job and then ask them to write a nice, detailed testimonial for you to place on your website (or copy and paste to send to people via email if you don't have a website yet). Make sure the testimonial includes some specifics showing how you actually helped them. If possible, you should also use some of the work in your portfolio if there are visible results, such as photos or videos you produce. If there are no visible, tangible end results (like with babysitting), that's OK.

Important Note: If you're creating a website for your service, be sure to use a separate website from your acting site. You should never advertise anything except your acting work on your main website (we'll be talking more about actor websites later).

Another fun thing to do is to get in the habit of asking your clients to take a selfie with you after a project is finished.

Then you'll have photos of actual people you helped (where you can attach the testimonial they wrote for you) to increase your credibility with new potential clients.

Reach out to 3-5 people you know who might need your services and offer to do the work for them one time for free in exchange for a testimonial, selfie with them, and permission to use the final product as an example of your work to show future clients.

Step 6: Start Finding Paid Clients on Craigslist

Craigslist is one of the best places to find clients fast for most services. The downside, however, is that most people on there are price shopping, meaning you'll have to keep your prices low to start. This is not always the case, however, so be sure not to drop your prices too low or people might get suspicious and think you're a scammer. The cool thing about Craigslist is that most of the freelancers responding to ads there are so unprofessional that even just replying with proper grammar and speaking in a professional tone of voice will put you heads and shoulders above the competition so you stand out.

Make it a habit to log into Craigslist each day to search for ads people post looking for your service. You'll respond to as many of these ads as possible and eventually start booking work (most likely within the first week or two). Plan on receiving one response for every five ads you reply to, and possibly more if you're sending highly personalized emails. Because you're just starting out though, you'll probably need to keep your rates somewhat low for the time being. You can start raising them once you get referral clients.

As a side note, some services might be more difficult to find opportunities for on Craigslist, so here are some other places you can use to find clients:

- **Life Coaching** - Networking events: if you offer a free session some people you meet will take you up on the offer and might become clients.

- **Martial Arts Instruction or Personal Training** - You can ask gyms if they have bulletin boards or places where you can put business cards and offer a free session with you. Some of these people might become clients.

- **Dance Classes or Acting Classes** - You can go to acting schools and leave your cards or post bulletin boards and offer a free class with you. Some of these people might become clients.

Here are a few general tips to get you the best response rates possible:

- **Make Things Easy** - Those hiring someone want a freelancer who can make it easy for them to hire and work with them. This all starts with the cover letter. Keeping your cover letter very short (less than 5 sentences) and readable while highlighting the two biggest benefits they'll get by hiring you is a good place to start. And then make it easy for them to interview you by showing up on time, being friendly, and showing them you're interested.

- **Expertise** - You should know a lot about the specific thing you are being hired to do. And if you aren't experienced, you need to show you are a quick learner and willing to do what it takes to get the job done properly. Remember though, having worked with at least 3-5 free clients beforehand should take care of this issue.

- **Look Friendly** - People usually feel much more comfortable hiring someone with a good photo of themselves showing a genuine smile. If you don't have a good photo of yourself (or you look mean in it), they might decide on someone else (I have literally not hired someone based on their headshot alone because they looked unfriendly and a bit creepy in it). A professional headshot can go a long way in establishing credibility, but you can also use a regular picture too.

- **Availability** - You should not be too needy in terms of working certain days or needing certain hourly minimums. The more desperate for cash or needy you seem, the less likely people will hire you because they'll worry you're going to be more of a liability than an asset.

- **Provides Added Value** - People hiring want someone who is able to provide them with even more value than they were expecting. If you have additional skills or personality traits that could be an asset in your job, make sure to point them out (more on this soon).

- **Cares About the Position** - You need to show that you really care about the job and can explain why you want it. People don't want you to work for them if it's just for the money because it means you won't do your best work. You have to really want it for the emotional reasons (enjoying the work) for someone to bring you on.

- **Honesty, Reliability, and Responsibility** - People who are honest and willing to be vulnerable are actually more likely to be selected. If you make a mistake and don't own up to it and apologize, but instead blame others, you won't get or keep the job. As someone who has hired many people, I see personal responsibility, honesty, and reliability as the top personality traits needed for great freelancers.

- **Calm and Relaxed** - In general, clients want to be sure that you're easy to work with. Some people I've hired in the past were on an emotional rollercoaster and it led to inappropriate outbursts at work and fights between employees which was bad for team morale. Most people want to hire someone who is generally cool, collected, calm, and rolls with the punches.

- **Unbeatable Guarantee** - If you can figure out a way to guarantee the client will get what they need, it makes it much easier for them to say yes to working with you. How can you guarantee a result to your client? Come up with something that doesn't make you too liable but also makes the client extremely willing to say yes.

Step 7: Turn on Your A-Player Sales Game

Sales is just the word to describe the part where you're actually talking to the client and they are considering whether to hire you. You need to have a plan of what you're going to say when they're emailing or on the phone with you so that you present yourself in the best possible light.

The best way to be successful in sales is, ironically, not to sell, but rather to be sold. Listen to your client's needs and ask questions to get them to explain to you what they most want. Ask them questions and then offer the best solution, custom-tailored to their needs.

Here are some additional tips you can use when talking to clients to increase their trust in you and make them want to hire you:

- **Show how easy you are to work with**. Explain that you're there for them and that you are great with rolling with the punches during projects. Let them know you're happy to help them with any needs they have in terms of project changes and requests, so long as they're reasonable.

- **Show how friendly you are**. When people talk to you, they aren't just looking for your experience. They want to talk to someone who seems friendly and shows interest in them rather than just talking about themselves and their accomplishments. If they ask about your experience tell them. But if they don't, keep the focus on them and their needs.

- **Dress and act professionally when you meet them**. Some people might be uncomfortable if you have a very intense wardrobe or personality. Keep things reserved and professional during the meeting so they feel comfortable with you.

- **Surprise them with some extra benefit**. What's something you can offer that would be super helpful to them, and that you can hide until you talk to them during your sales meeting or consultation? If you can mention it at that time as a surprise, they will be more likely to hire you (as long as they actually care about it). Example: You offer general babysitting services, but surprise them during your consultation by saying you are also an excellent cook and can make their kids healthy meals at night for no extra charge if they supply the ingredients.

- **Show that you care about the position**. Explain why you want to work with them and why you love doing this type of work so much. People want to hire freelancers who are passionate about what they do, and even if you're not 100% passionate about babysitting, you should at least figure out 2-3 things you love about it so you come off as more excited when speaking to potential clients.

- **Be professional**. Ensure you're on time to your meeting or slightly early, and keep your clients updated if you're running slightly late (but try not to be late because regardless of the excuse, it's a huge turn off). Also be sure that your emails are well-written with proper spelling and grammar because that can be an instant turn off as well in many people's books.

- **Bring up their problems before they bring them up**. During your sales pitch, show you understand their predicament by explaining to them exactly what their problems are before they even tell them to you themselves. *Example: In the babysitting situation, you can say that you understand how most moms are worried their babysitters don't pay full attention to their kids and just sit on their phones all evening. Then you'll tell them how you like to pay extra attention to kids to make sure they are getting the care they need. You can follow up by telling them how much you've always loved interacting with children.* Articulating their problems or worries better than they can will build even more trust.

Step 8: Under-promise and over-deliver by making it easy.

Once someone actually hires you, it's time to do you absolute best. Remember what most people value - responsiveness, ease of working with you, friendliness, good customer service, a high-quality product, etc. Make sure that you over deliver on each of those.

One of the most effective ways to get people to absolutely love working with you is to make everything as easy as possible for the client. Your goal should be that all the client has to do is say, "Yeah, sounds good!" If you do this consistently, you'll have a line of clients begging to hire you.

Example: If I'm hiring a babysitter, I would love it if the babysitter just sent me an email saying, "So I know you're leaving at 6pm Tuesday night to go out to the show. I'd be happy to arrive by 5:45pm to get settled if that works, and I can pick up some dinner for the kids if you want on my way over (perhaps sandwiches from Justin's Deli). Does that work?" And then all I would have to say is, "Yeah, sounds good!"

No one wants to work with someone who puts all the heavy lifting on them. It's way more challenging for me to have to deal with a babysitter who says, "Ok, so you're leaving at 6pm. What time do you want me to come?" And then I would have to say a time and then it's a whole bunch of back and forth with a number of emails figuring out if the babysitter should bring food, etc. I'd much rather work with a person who makes it easy and suggests things they think are best for me. That's when I feel I'm working with someone really awesome. And that's the type of person I'm going to constantly refer to my friends!

Step 9: Build referrals and start raising your rates.

Now that you're treating your clients like they're the most important people in the world to you (because they should be), it's time to start generating referrals. Ask your clients whether they know anyone else who might be able to use your services. Without asking them, they won't suggest anyone. The worst that could happen is they tell you they don't know anyone! If they mention any names to you though, you can reach out to those people and offer a free consultation.

As you begin bringing in clients through referral business, you'll be able to start raising your rates slowly. Each new client you work with is a chance to increase your rates a little bit because referral business usually pays more than the people you find on Craigslist or through ads.

But it's vitally important that you make sure to keep your end goal in mind: How much money do you want to be making each month and how much free time do you need to be able to pursue your acting career? If your acting career is important, don't let your side hustle cause you to lose sight of your dream.

By keeping the end goal in mind, you'll ensure you're moving in the right direction so that pretty soon (most likely within 6-9 months), you'll be able to quit whatever full-time or part-time job you have and just use the money from your side hustle to pay your bills while you spend your free time pursuing acting!

Be Careful of What You Sign

Do you read contracts? I can't stress this enough. If you don't read the contracts you sign into, that's basically like giving someone you've never met the keys to your car and saying, "I trust you to hold onto these because I don't feel like carrying them around today."

Don't do it!

Read through every contract you sign if you don't have an agent or lawyer and can't afford one. Remember that unless you have actually fully looked over a legitimate contract before, you won't know what you are signing into or what is being left out. Ask questions or look things up online if you don't understand them.

Watch out for the word "indemnify." If that word is in the contract, be sure you know what you are indemnifying the company from. This means that you are saying that if something goes wrong, you are indemnifying - or protecting - the other side from any lawsuits. You don't want to be held responsible if the company is sued by someone for copyright infringement, because that wasn't your fault! But if you signed a contract that says you agree to indemnify them from all lawsuits, you're on the line, even if it wasn't your fault at all!

Fortunately as the person being asked to sign the agreement, you generally have the upper hand. This means that unless it's in the contract, you are usually not obligated. For instance if you signed a contract saying the film company had the rights to use your appearance in the film but said nothing about a trailer, you could sue them as soon as they used your face in a trailer, because the film is separate from the trailer. Obviously you shouldn't be suing filmmakers if you want to be a successful actor, but you get the idea.

Now, even though you have the upper hand in contracts, you still absolutely must read everything and potentially consult a lawyer before signing into anything that you aren't sure about. What if the contract stated you would only be paid after twenty years? You never know, but if you sign and it comes up in court, you can't win that case because the judge will just say, "You signed into that agreement!"

Lastly, be sure that you always get a copy of the contract. Many actors forget to ask for a copy, but you want to make sure you have it for your records. How can you fight a lawsuit if you sign something but don't have a copy of it to prove it to the judge? What if the production company changed the wording in it and pretended you signed something different? Always get a copy of the contract before you leave. If there are no copies around, take photos of every page of the contract with your smartphone.

Disclaimer: I am not a lawyer, so don't take the advice in this section (or anywhere else in this book) as legal advice. Consult a licensed attorney for that!

Checking Your Online Reputation

Now that you've figured out what you really want in your acting career, the character types you're most suited for, what shows or films you're hoping to target, and you've got your money situation under control, it's time to start taking real action to move your acting career forward.

The first thing you'll need to do to for success is remove anyone's doubts about hiring you.

Go online and search your name in quotation marks like *"Martin Bentsen"* or *"Martin Bentsen" actor*. If you find way too much stuff because you have a common name, adding the word "actor" outside of the quotation marks can help bring up stuff only related to your acting career (though you might want to consider using a more specific stage name down the line so others can find you more easily).

Delete any bad/old acting reels you find and just keep the good ones. No one cares to see the bad/old projects you acted in unless they are your really close friends or they were in the project themselves. And those people probably already have access to those projects, either by having their own copy or through you.

Remove them from your website, YouTube, or ask directors/producers to remove your name from their websites if you don't want them showing up in search results of your name in the future.

It's imperative you manage your reputation like this because you only want your potential employers (i.e. casting directors) to see your best stuff.

Also, be sure to take a look at your social media accounts and remove anything you've posted in the past that could be frowned upon by people in the industry. If you wouldn't want your grandma seeing it, you probably don't want casting directors or agents to see it!

Finally, I recommend setting up a Google Alert for yourself. Visit www.google.com/alerts and you'll be able to set up an automation where any time something shows up online with your name attached, you'll receive an email letting you know.

Talk about a simple way to monitor your online reputation, don't you love technology?

Part 4: Create Your Basic Marketing Materials

You've spent all this time getting organized, figuring out what you really want, and preparing yourself for success, and we're halfway through this book!

Most actors skip everything in the prepping stage and wonder why they get stuck. They don't think about what makes them unique, they don't figure out what they really want, and they don't set themselves up to be financially secure.

But since you've done all the hard work, things are now going to get really fun and a bit easier.

In this section we'll be discussing your headshot and resume, we'll talk about how to get good footage of yourself online, and we'll also go into detail on how to effectively use those marketing tools to move your career forward.

Four Quick Marketing To-Do's

You've spent so much time thinking and preparing that you're probably itching to do some real work. So here are a few quick things you can do right away to jump ahead:

1. **Set up a URL with your first and last name in it** - Something like www.martinbentsen.com. You could also use the word "actor" in your URL if your name is already taken, like www.martinbentsenactor.com. Check out www.martinbentsen.com/get-cast to see suggestions of some websites where you can purchase your own domain name.

2. **Create business cards with your headshot, name, website, and email address** - for my most up to date recommendations on where to order business cards, visit www.martinbentsen.com/get-cast. Try to make sure the look of your business cards aligns with your brand, and if you're not sure how, ask a designer to help you (some recommendations of graphic designers are also listed on my members-only site). Don't buy more than 250 business cards right now, because chances are you might want to change them over the course of the coming year.

3. **Go through your emails from a long time ago and make a list in Excel** - Find all the people in your industry you knew personally and liked. Include their

name, phone number, and email, along with a note on how you knew them, and put them into a simple Excel sheet so you can easily find their contact info at any point if you need it. We'll be referencing this contact list later on.

4. **Create a free YouTube account** - If you don't already have one, I recommend checking out www.youtube.com and setting up an account there. YouTube is a great platform to upload footage of yourself as you start to get clips. I usually recommend YouTube over other platforms such as Vimeo because YouTube videos are easier to embed onto websites and it has much more traffic, meaning more people will stumble across your clips.

Upgrade Your Headshots

Is your current headshot professional and does it capture your brand? If you don't have one, it's time to book a shoot. If you do, take it out and think about a few things:

1. Was it taken professionally? If you're not sure, just google "professional actor headshots" and look at some of the samples that come up - you'll get an idea right away of what constitutes a professional headshot. You can also visit actors.cityheadshots.com to see some examples.

2. Does it speak to your brand? When you look at your headshot, are your Pride Words & character type clear?

3. Have you gotten many auditions from it?

4. Do other people you know in the industry think it's good?

5. Do you look the same in real life as you do in the shot?

6. Does it look like an expensive headshot? Or does it look like you had a friend take your picture?

7. Are you happy with it?

If the answer to any of those questions is no, then it's time to get some new headshots taken.

Remember that the key to being called into auditions is your headshot. You need to project confidence and look like you can act. Here some tips to get an amazing headshot:

1. **Wear to your shoot what you love to wear** - If you choose to bring things you think look more professional or better than what you feel comfortable in, you might not look relaxed in the headshot because it's not really you.

2. **Remember that it takes time to get into the mood** - You won't get good headshots until you've had time to get used to the photographer and are hitting it off well. If you're joking around and in a great mood, you'll get a great headshot. As soon as you start losing the good mood or connection with the photographer, your shots won't come out as good.

3. **Have fun** - It's important to have a good time. Think about happy and fun memories if the photographer can't get you there. A good headshot photographer should be able to direct you into the right expression, but if they have trouble, then it's up to you because you want awesome shots and are already paying them. Just be happy, confident and have fun!

4. **Don't step too far out of your comfort zone** - Don't do things that will make you feel awkward, like wearing something new before the headshot session or

trying new makeup. If you're worried about how you look, it will show in your expressions.

You definitely don't have to spend thousands of dollars for a good headshot, but before hiring someone, you should thoroughly research them. Be sure that the photographer will be able to provide the following things:

1. **Great lighting -** You need great lighting that makes your face pop off the image. It has to really make you stand out from the background.

2. **A nice non-distracting background -** An extremely blurry or flat background - something that supports the type of character you are going for and doesn't draw too much attention away from your face - is ideal. Check out www.martinbentsen.com/get-cast for additional resources on what colored backdrops and types of shots work for different brands and acting styles.

3. **A shot that captures your brand -** A single headshot should not be used for all submissions. You want a few different looks that you can send out for each role, so your photographer should be able to capture specific aspects of your brand in each shot. Earlier, we came up with the example brand: *The strong, driven, and passionate father who can be violent at times.* Aim for a shot such like "strong and driven father" or "violent father." Avoid trying to

capture more than two emotions at once in a shot because it can be confusing for people looking at the image. Casting directors don't want to use their imagination, so you should be very specific with each shot.

The easiest way to capture a professional and memorable headshot is to show genuine emotion with a real expression. Think about emotionally connecting with the viewer so people remember your shot and wonder who you are, and why your expression looked like that. Then they'll want to meet you.

The above points are essential to getting a good headshot, so be sure your photographer can capture those things. If you'd like to work with me or my team personally, check out actors.cityheadshots.com.

Finding a Great Photographer

Remember, money is not always skill. Sometimes someone who is a natural at headshot photography and is just getting started in the business can give you great headshots for a low price! But always look at their portfolio first, because you don't want to spend even $50 if the headshots you get back are useless. Remember what I mentioned earlier about unprofessional headshots costing you THOUSANDS of dollars in missed opportunities?

After looking at a photographer's headshot samples, give them a call (assuming they're in your price range). You can email them but it's a better idea to call because you want to get an idea of what kind of person they are by talking to them over the phone, especially if you can't tell their personality from their website.

Do they (or their assistant) have time for you? Do they even care? Don't work with them if they don't seem to be interested in talking to you, or seem too busy to want to deal with you.

Email to set up a time, and be sure they are responsive. This goes for any professional you might be working with: if they take more than 1-2 business days to respond, that's not a good sign. You need to always feel comfortable knowing that your headshot photographer is prepared and ready to serve you. You're paying them, so why should you be worried that they might not show up?

If you can set up an in-person consultation with them, that's great, but many headshot photographers are very busy and can't offer their time like that, so if that is not an option, you needn't worry too much. If it is an option, however, it can be a good way to get to know them better and see if you get along well. The headshot photographer should be able to make you laugh and you should feel comfortable around him/her, as it is the only way you will get good pictures.

On the day of the shoot, the best thing to do is to take things lightly and not be worried about trying to get the perfect shot, because it will happen if you give the photographer enough time and you two get along well.

Be sure to ask the photographer for references if they don't have a website with good photos on it. Don't get scammed by someone asking exorbitant sums of money or weird payment plans (although keep in mind that most photographers will charge a booking deposit to reserve the session date, and this money is typically applied to the shoot total).

You shouldn't need to pay much more than $600 for a headshot, and if you are ever paying more than $1,200, it's because you are probably shooting with a well-known photographer, and in that case they should be offering you value beyond just the headshot, such as helping you choose the best images, providing retouched photos, etc. Remember, if something sounds suspicious, it's probably a scam.

What to Wear in Your Headshots

What to wear actually starts with you as the actor. What is your brand, and what would that character wear? You should do at least one look with what you'd wear on a regular day as yourself, and one look that's very specifically focused on your brand and type. Example: What would a *strong, driven, and passionate father who can get violent at times* wear?

The clothing you wear coupled with the expression on your face is going to be what will sell your headshot to casting directors. When you decide on clothing, pick things that will bring out the different characters you are good at playing, and the characters you want to audition for. But also be sure that you love the clothes you're going to wear. Don't just pick something you think the character would look good wearing if you're uncomfortable in it. You won't feel comfortable in clothes you don't love, and looking natural on camera is key.

For general guidelines, be sure to wear darker colors if you are dark-skinned, and medium colors if you are light-skinned. Shy away from really pale colors, like yellow, pink, light blue, and white as the main layers. Deeper colors look best. Wear layers for interest (jackets work really well).

Don't wear plaid or any crazy patterns. Try to keep it simple - mostly solid-colored shirts. For instance, a light blue shirt with a dark brown jacket would look good. Don't wear shirts with logos or brand names, and wear a color you look good in. Try to keep it simple and try to look like you usually look. Don't go crazy or your headshot will wind up looking weird. Avoid jewelry.

If you want a much more detailed guide on what colors to wear and how to prepare for a headshot session, check out www.martinbentsen.com/get-cast.

Lastly, get a professional makeup artist if possible. They'll know how to do your makeup for camera in a natural way that will work best for actor headshots. And remember, you want a makeup artist who does makeup specifically for headshots, which is different than day to day makeup or glamour makeup for a special event. A makeup artist will also make sure your face isn't shiny in the photos, your clothing is in place, and that your hair is looking good if it's windy and you're shooting outside.

Start Using Your New Headshots

Once you've gotten your headshots taken, there are a number of ways you can use them besides the standard 8x10 prints. The more places you post them, the more memorable you'll be!

1. **Your website homepage** - Place your headshot on the main page of your website so that the first thing people see is your headshot. It allows visitors to feel a connection to you and get a better sense of who you are. Photos have been proven to increase memorability and connection, especially color photos of faces with a strong and genuine emotion. If you don't have a website yet, you can skip this step.

2. **Personal profiles** - Place your headshot on everything else you have online, such as your blog, Facebook page, and other social networking sites.

3. **IMDB and IBDB** - Place your headshot on your IMDB page and IBDB page (to be able to do this, you must upgrade to IMDB or IBDB Pro).

4. **Online casting websites** - Post your headshots on all the acting sites you have profiles on, like "Mandy," "Actor's Access," "Backstage," and others.

5. **LinkedIn** - Put your headshot on your LinkedIn page. Don't have a LinkedIn page? Get one immediately

because even though you're in a creative industry, casting directors, agents, and hiring managers still use LinkedIn to look up actors. LinkedIn isn't just for corporate people. Artists need a page too if they want to appear established, trustworthy, and professional.

6. **Business cards and postcards** - Get business cards and postcards made with your headshots printed on them. Business cards are great because you can walk around all day with them and not even think about it until someone asks you for your info and you hand them a card with your picture. The same goes for a postcard print. A postcard print is about 3.5 by 5 inches and has four or five different photos of you on it. Be sure your headshot is on whatever you hand people so they can easily remember who you are.

Feel free to ask your friends and other actors you know if they use their headshots in creative ways, and take note if you ever come across someone who uses them in a unique way. The more places your headshot is, the more familiar people will become with your face, and the more likely you'll be top of mind when an opportunity comes - this way they'll remember to reach out to you!

Create a Strong Resume

Have you ever sent out hundreds of resumes to auditions, agents, or managers and not heard back?

I know the feeling. I remember a few years ago I was doing a promotion for my company City Headshots, and I sent out cold emails to over 300 people.

I wasn't sending my resume per se, but I was sending a brief writeup on our company and some of its biggest achievements - an email aimed at bringing in more business.

I sent out the email and waited to hear back, excited for all the opportunities about to come.

The next morning I woke up. I checked my email.

One new response!

I opened it.

"Don't email me again."

...

Seriously?

That really hurt... I had spent over two hours drafting my email and sending it to specific people in the industry I thought would be interested. And all I got back was a single, rude response from one person.

Sending out so many resumes and headshots for auditions and rarely hearing back can be a huge blow to your confidence, so I want to discuss some simple ways your resume could be hurting your chances for success.

What is it that makes the difference between someone responding to your submission and not?

Well, I learned the answer a few months later when I sent cold emails out to 50 people and received positive, excited responses back from 11 (a 22% response rate is pretty good)!

The difference? My second email campaign focused on the client and what was in it for them.

A resume that doesn't show "what's in it for them" could be costing you more than you think.

First off, your resume needs to be properly laid out in a professional "actor resume" format. It should be easy on the eyes to anyone looking at it. Make sure it's only 1-page!

Eventually you can make your resume fancy like some of the ones you can find by googling "actor resume sample," but when you're first starting out you should keep things simple.

Below are a few key points to keep in mind for an effective actor resume that focuses on "what's in it for them":

• Include your contact information.

- Include your website domain name (again, visit www.martinbentsen.com/get-cast for my suggestions on where you can purchase a domain name).

- The largest and most noteworthy projects you've been in.

- Any noteworthy education you have, especially your training.

- Any special skills you have.

- Make sure to use the words "lead" and "supporting" etc., instead of character names, especially for film and TV roles.

- Leave out minor things that aren't important - they might make it look like you're just trying to fill up space.

- Put the most relevant things first - if you're focus is film, don't put your theater work on your resume unless you need to fill up space.

- Remember that casting directors can easily tell if you're padding your resume or lying, so don't do it.

Keep in mind that casting directors and agents are super busy. They are interested in seeing your experience as quickly as possible and finding out whatever special skills you have. Make it easy for them to find these things.

TIP 1: Lead vs. Supporting

Some people ask why I recommend using the words "lead" and "supporting" instead of character names, and the reason is simple: casting directors don't know every single project out there and won't spend the time to go look them up, so avoid using character names, especially for films and television shows!

As a filmmaker myself, it's way easier and appreciated when actors submit resumes to me that list the type of role they played instead of the character name because I can tell right away how much experience they have.

TIP 2: Doc vs. PDF

Another important thing to remember is that you should NEVER send out .doc format resumes. ALWAYS send out a PDF file because .doc files reformat on different computers, meaning your one-page resume might show up as two pages somewhere else.

Doc formats can also sometimes contain viruses, so casting directors can be leery when opening them. If you're not sure how to make PDF files, you can just google it (different articles exist for different computer operating systems like Mac vs Windows).

TIP 3: Small Resume? No Worries.

What do you do if you have no experience and your resume is tiny? Well, as they say - if you build it they will come. As we discussed earlier, you gotta start acting for free to build your resume! Apply to casting calls for student films and ultra-low budget productions to start getting credits.

Casting directors and agents rarely take on inexperienced actors for big projects that will be shown to large audiences because the risk is too great, so prepare to spend at least 3-6 months acting for free before your resume starts looking better and you start booking professional paid work.

Get Some Sort of Footage of Yourself Online

If you already have a fantastic demo reel you're 100% proud of, this section is probably not for you.

But if you think your reel could use an update (or you don't have any footage yet), keep reading. By the end of this part, you'll be clear on exactly what you can do to get footage fast.

So let's jump right in.

There are four primary ways you can get more footage for your reel:

1. Act in student films and low-budget productions for free.

2. Write, direct, and shoot your own short film (and act in it).

3. Have a friend use a smartphone to get footage of you performing.

4. Shoot a professional scene for your reel.

Let's go over each of the ways, along with the benefits and pitfalls of each.

Act in Student Films and Low-Budget Productions for Free

The benefits to student films are that they're a bit easier to get cast in than professional projects (especially if they're unpaid), and they're also a great way to gain experience on set and make connections.

The downside, however, is that even though they might be slightly easier to get cast in, there are still TONS of actors out there vying for these unpaid roles, so you need to audition really well and have a great headshot that captures the attention of the filmmaker. We'll discuss audition technique later.

Another thing to keep in mind is that with student films, it can take many months to get your footage back from directors, and once you do get it back, you might be disappointed that the quality isn't that good.

Keep in mind, however, that when you're first starting, the quality of the footage in your reel is far less important than being able to clearly see and hear you on camera. Casting directors just want to see what you look like and feel confident in your ability to act. They're not as worried if your footage doesn't look super high-end.

So all in all, acting for free in student projects can definitely be a viable way to get footage, especially if you chat with the director ahead of time and ensure they will be giving you access to your footage right away.

Write, Direct, and Act in Your Own Project

Making your own films and projects can be fun and exciting. If all you do is act in other people's projects, you won't have as much control. But imagine if you wrote, directed, and starred in your own short film or play. How would that look to a casting director?

Seeing that you have such an interest in film and acting will impress a lot of people, and they will likely give your resume a second look, which increases your chances of being called in.

Note: Whenever you act in a theater production, see if you can get a portion of your performance filmed. It's impossible to put samples of your work online if you have never recorded them, right? So ask a friend to recording some of your performances with your smartphone. Or set a camera up on a tripod. This is easier when it's your own project though because some directors won't allow you to record any of the performance.

The downside of creating and shooting your own projects is that way too many people start to put them together and then realize how much work it is, and they wind up never finishing. Don't let that be you.

There are literally millions of actors competing for only a few roles. If you have something like a completed, professional short film, or a great theater piece that you wrote, directed, recorded, and uploaded to the Internet, you'll put yourself ahead of many other actors.

If you get a great DP (director of photography), you can walk away with some outstanding footage of yourself, and you'll have access to it immediately.

The biggest downside of course, besides the fact that you'll need to learn how to write, direct, produce, and hire people, is that there is an enormous cost if you don't already have all the needed equipment.

Even for a short film, you're likely to spend at least $3k altogether. You need to pay people, buy food, get permits and insurance, rent equipment, and much more.

Now don't get me wrong - if you already know the right people and can get everyone to work for free, I've seen short films that look great and were done for less than $1,000 - but you need an extraordinary level of knowledge and lots of friends willing to work for free (plus access to free locations that don't require insurance).

Do you think you can do it completely free? It's possible but highly unlikely. The small costs quickly add up - between paying for food and transportation (plus the hard drives to back your footage up on), you're probably going to spend at least $500-1,000 if you want quality good enough to use in your acting reel.

Making your own short film is definitely possible but takes a lot of knowledge and expertise to pull off, so do your homework and be prepared for Murphy's Law (anything that can go wrong will go wrong)!

Have a Friend Record You Performing

Now that you know the pitfalls of making your own film and the downsides of acting for free in student films, having a friend record you with a smartphone is probably starting to look like the best option.

The clear benefits are that you'll get immediate access to your footage, it costs virtually nothing (unless your friend is a jerk and charges you), and you don't need any expertise (unless you have no idea how to use an iPhone).

Casting directors don't mind looking at these "self-tapes" because they give them a good idea of your on-camera acting ability.

The only downside is that if this is the only footage you have, it could tell casting directors that you have limited on-set experience, which might make them leery of bringing you in (especially for bigger projects).

Regardless of that downside, I highly recommend starting with this option if you have absolutely zero footage, need something right away, and are very short on funds.

Shoot a Professional Scene for Your Reel

I'm sure you've heard the saying in the acting industry:

"There's money, time, and quality. But you can only have two."

So here are your three options:

1. You can save money and have a great quality footage for your reel, but it's going to take a long time.

2. You can save money and time, but you'll have crappy footage.

3. You can save time and have great footage, but you'll have to spend money.

If you want great quality footage for your reel and you want that footage fast, invest a little money in yourself and pay for a highly-professional, customized scene shot for your demo reel.

There are numerous reel production companies, but if you work with Actor Screener Shoot, you'll get access to all your footage within a week of the shoot (fully edited, sound-mixed, and color-graded) and you'll be able to start sending it out to casting directors immediately.

Check out www.actorscreenershoot.com to learn about this special service my team offers for actors.

Part 5: Start Submitting

Are you ready to start getting paid for your acting work and booking bigger and better roles than you ever have? Since you've done all the planning and you've created your basic marketing materials, it's now time to go out there and make things happen.

In this section, we're going to talk about how to find the right auditions, how to submit for them, how to knock them out of the park, and how to interact and network with people in the industry in such a way that makes them want to keep working with you over and over again.

And if you have NOT yet read Parts 1, 2, and 3, I strongly advise you to go back and do so. Your submissions process and auditions will be WAY more effective if you've done the proper preparation beforehand.

Do your homework to get your A!

Start Finding Auditions Online

It's time to dive into acting and start turning your dreams into reality. In this section, we'll be talking about how to find auditions and self-submit. Even if you already have an agent or manager, self-submissions are going to help you find more opportunities. Don't sit around and wait for your agent or manager to submit you - you can do it yourself too!

To start off, create profiles on each of the main online casting websites. A full listing of sites can be found at www.martinbentsen.com/get-cast.

If you've been going through this book in order, you'll have already written out the ideal roles you'd love to play. You should have at least three specific roles you're going to focus on.

You'll also have a list of about 10 plays, films, or TV shows you'd like to be a part of. It's now time to decide which projects you want to focus your submissions on.

Think about projects you've submitted for in the past and ones that you will submit for now. What types of projects should you NO LONGER be submitting for? Write down a list and get clear on the ones you should avoid.

Don't just think of genres and character types as your criteria. You can also think of projects you've been involved in that turned out to be big challenges or had crew members that were a pain to work with.

Create a checklist for yourself of projects you won't submit for anymore. Here's an example:

I will no longer submit to the following types of projects:

- Unpaid projects unless it's for a charitable cause

- Projects that don't fulfill me or connect with my brand

- Projects with directors that give me an uneasy feeling

- Projects where the online casting call has numerous spelling errors and doesn't seem very professional

- Etc.

Remember - the more you avoid the wrong projects, the more time and focus you'll have for the RIGHT projects, which means you'll do better work on those. Doing your best work leads to referrals and stronger, long term contacts in the industry.

Now it's time to start submitting yourself online to projects that will support building a reel dedicated specifically to booking the roles you want. Look for any breakdowns that specifically support your brand and the character types you want to play and self-submit!

Submit yourself to at least 10 projects that are perfect over the next seven days.

The Importance of Craving Criticism

As you begin to self-submit, you're inevitably going to come across people who criticize your performance and don't do it in the most tactful way.

Regardless of how the criticism sounds, it's your job to always be open to it if you want success. Casting directors and directors are going to give you feedback and it's always your job to turn what they ask for into tangible results.

Directors want to hire someone who is easy to work with and will respond well to direction, and no one will want to work with you if you aren't easy to work with.

If you can take anyone's feedback well (again, even if it sounds harsher than you'd like), you're going to create more long-term opportunities for yourself.

And don't get annoyed if people criticize other things about you outside of the audition room. Listening to critique and thanking people for it will make them more open to giving you feedback in the future, and negative feedback is one of the fastest ways to learn new things about yourself that can help you become better in the long run.

If you know someone's feedback is wrong, you should still thank them and show you appreciate their feedback - there's no benefit in trying to say they're wrong. Always look for any nuggets of truth you can find because negative feedback is one of the fastest ways to improve.

What Goes into a Great Cover Letter

When self-submitting, you're going to have a really hard time getting in the room if you're not perfect for the part. Take a look at these numbers:

On average, about 3,000 actors submit for every professional audition. The casting director usually has about 30 slots available for auditions, and most will already have 5-10 actors they want to bring in (and the director might have a couple too). This leaves 20 slots for 3000 actors. That's less than a 1% chance of being called in.

So how do join that top 1%? Here are four ways you can stand out:

1. **A highly-professional headshot that captures your brand in a way that resonates with the casting director** - Typically only about 20% of actors that submit use a professional headshot that looks like the character the casting director is searching for. That drops the submission pool down to 600 actors.

2. **A well-formatted PDF version of your resume with at least a few relevant credits** - Typically only 25% of the remaining actors who submit have a resume that's tailored to the character type they're submitting for. This narrows the pool down further to about 150 actors for the audition.

3. **Footage of themselves with great film acting technique** - Usually most actors who submit a professional resume and headshot will include some sort of footage. But typically only half have great film acting skills. So now we're down to about 75 qualified applicants.

4. **A well-written, short and engaging cover letter that captures the attention of the casting director and makes them interested in meeting the actor** - Only about 10% of the remaining actors will take this extra step. That drops it down to about 7 or 8 final actors, perfect to fill in some of those 20 available slots.

Since a strong cover letter can absolutely help you stand out and is such an easy thing to create (unlike building a resume or reel), I've put together a simple guide you can use to ensure it catches the casting director's attention. First, take a look at the sample cover letter that can be found at www.martinbentsen.com/get-cast. Then follow the tips below:

It Must Be Branded

First off, ensure that your cover letter talks a bit about what types of characters you most enjoy playing and why. It's important to remember that casting directors are not just looking for an actor that LOOKS like the role, but they're also looking for an actor who LOVES playing that kind of role.

They know that when you love doing something, you'll do your best work. For this reason, casting directors are rarely going to hire an actor with a generic brand - they'll think that they're just "eh" about their project.

Show how you're perfect for the project because the character is your exact brand and you're experienced in it and absolutely love playing it.

It Must Be Short

A good cover letter should be only 3-5 sentences, broken up into 3 short paragraphs. Any longer and no one will read it.

A wise man named Charles Mingus once said, "Making the simple complex is commonplace. But making the complex simple, awesomely simple - that's creativity."

It's your job to figure out how to condense your cover letter down to about 4 sentences while covering all the most important points.

It Must Show the Value You Bring to the Table

Casting directors care about the brand you play and that it matches the character they are auditioning for, but they also care about what you'll bring the project outside of your acting ability.

In this sense, we're primarily talking about your attitude and how you interact with other people on projects.

It's beneficial to talk a bit about how you're a positive person, you love working with people as a team, and you always strive to help others feel good about themselves. Showing you're a supportive, positive person can go further than you'd think in bringing you in for an audition.

Why? Because casting directors like to hire team players.

It Must Be Professional

You'd be surprised to see how many actors don't know proper grammar or how to spell correctly.

If you have a friend who's great at English, ask them to double-check your cover letters before they go out because it can go a long way in showing your professionalism.

When you cross all your T's and dot all your I's, casting directors and agents will think you are a true professional. And when you send out an unprofessional cover letter, it shows that you let things fall through the cracks.

Read more about professionalism in the next section.

Be Professional to Stand Out

In an industry where many actors send out emails with spelling errors, don't respond quickly enough, and show up late to auditions, you'll stand out by being professional.

Here are six things to keep in mind as you start connecting and networking with people in the industry:

1. **Use proper grammar.** Sending emails with bad grammar or spelling errors is a huge turn off. Be sure to use spell check software, but don't depend on it 100% because sometimes it's wrong! If you have a friend who is really great at spelling and grammar, ask them to review important things before sending them out.

2. **Always respond to emails and messages promptly.** Don't delay! Return phone calls and respond to emails within 12 hours. The only excuse for not returning a message is if you are going somewhere and don't have access to the Internet. If this is the case, set up an auto-responder and a voicemail telling people when you'll be back. Messages not responded to within one day are often viewed by potential employers as not important to you, so why would they hire someone who thinks their company or project is not important?

3. **Arrive on time or early.** It is not stylish to arrive to an appointment fashionably late, it's just rude. If you arrive even a few minutes after your scheduled arrival

time, you aren't being professional. The converse is also true. Don't arrive to an audition or interview 45 minutes early and expect them to take you right then. That's just as rude as arriving late because they aren't ready for you yet.

4. **Don't be afraid to make phone calls.** If you're not willing to call people you don't know well because you're nervous and think texting and emailing is easier, you're not sending the right message. I know many people who feel awkward making calls and opt to use written messages instead. People in this industry almost always need to speak over the phone if it's something urgent, and they don't like to deal with actors who just email or text back instead of returning a call. But the same actually goes for written messages: if someone emails you and doesn't ask you to call them back, don't. Don't just call someone because you see they emailed you. Chances are they emailed you because they are too busy to call you, and if you insist on calling them all the time you might risk annoying them.

5. **Use a professional email address.** Don't use something like bootyliciousxoxo@gmail.com. That's terribly unprofessional. Remember, you're likely going to be judged by your email address, and you shouldn't use something like sexman101@aol.com unless you're applying for a job as a porn star. Keep it simple like your.name@gmail.com, and make sure you check your emails at least 2-3 times per day.

6. **Use a professional and friendly voicemail greeting.** Don't use something like, "What's up guys, I'm not here right now, but you know what to do!" because it will definitely result in nobody except your friends calling you again. Same with something like: "Leave a message." A voicemail greeting like this makes it seem like you think you're better than the person calling and that they aren't worth your time. Try, "Hi, you've reached [your name here], professional actor and voiceover artist. I'm unable to answer the phone right now, but if you leave me a message and the best number to reach you at, I'll get back to you as soon as possible."

An Easy Fix to Get Called In More Often

Occasionally I'll send an email out to everyone on my mailing list asking for actors to send me their headshot and reel for some sort of opportunity such as being in an Actor Screener Shoot or submitting to an audition we're holding.

I'll often mention that we won't consider actors for the part unless they send over their headshot and/or reel.

I'll always get at least a few people who respond and say they would like to be considered for the opportunity, and to send them more info and shooting dates.

This would be fine, except the problem is... the shooting date and info was already included in my original email where I asked them to submit their headshot, and they didn't even include their headshot!

As basic as it sounds, when it comes to submitting for audition opportunities, make sure to read the whole casting notice and follow exact directions.

Casting directors use more ways than just looking at your headshot, resume, and cover letter to determine whether you're right for a project. Sometimes they ask very specific questions or request certain things just to see if you're paying attention - or in other words, if you care enough about their project to read EVERY line.

Occasionally I'll get a message from an actor saying they can't submit their reel or headshot right now because it's on a different computer or they don't have it handy.

But what if someone offers you a great opportunity to meet an agent and you're out of town for a week? Will you be unable to send them those basic marketing materials?

Make sure that you at least have your website URL handy so you can quickly write up a short cover letter and include a link to your website. Then you can say that your reel, resume, and headshot can be found there. And again, if you don't have your website yet, we'll get there soon enough.

What are Casting Directors Looking For?

This is one of the most common questions I get from actors as a marketing coach. What do casting directors really want from actors? What's the secret sauce they're looking for?

Well in this section, I'm going to go into great depth on the exact hiring process most casting directors use, and I'm also going to explain *why* casting directors don't want to give you too much information up front.

So what do they really want?

Unfortunately, we'll never know for sure.

I'm sure this is NOT the answer you were hoping for, but the truth is, every casting director is looking for something slightly different., and they're never going to be perfectly clear in the casting call because they don't want people to use the information they post to try to manipulate themselves into being selected for the audition.

What do I mean? Well, let's take a moment and pretend I'm looking to hire a new photographer for City Headshots.

If I wrote in the job description that what I'm most looking for is a photographer who chats a lot with the client as they shoot, EVERYONE will write "I love to chat while I shoot" in their cover letter or application (even though most of them are probably lying and don't actually do that).

Now I've just made it way more difficult to sort through the applications and find the people who really do chat with the client while they shoot.

And I ONLY want people who do it already and don't need to be told ahead of time because chatting while you shoot is hard! It takes years of training, so even if you were applying and knew I wanted you to chat while you were shooting, you'd have a hard time doing it during the test shoot, and I just wasted 20 minutes of my time with you.

Or if I somehow wound up hiring you because you *faked* your way through the test shoot by chatting a lot, chances are high that when it comes time to work in my company for real, you wouldn't chat with clients much because you're not used to doing it.

It's the same with actors - if you're not already a certain personality type or character, chances are you won't play that role as well as someone who is a natural.

So if there were 3,000 actors who submitted for a project, and the casting director told them all EXACTLY what he/she wanted to see, it would make their job of narrowing submissions down WAY harder because everyone would tell them what they wanted to hear.

They ONLY want people who *naturally* fit the role. Even if you knew EXACTLY what a casting director wanted, you'd never be as natural/skilled at playing it as an actor whose natural personality (and brand) matched what they were looking for.

Casting directors *only* want to compare the best of the best during the audition - they don't want all the other actors who are just putting on a show.

So you see, by only giving basic information, it's easier to see who is *naturally* the right fit, instead having to worry about being duped in the audition by those that *fake* it.

The Casting Process, Step by Step

Here is the process casting directors follow when looking to audition actors:

1. **Post the casting call** - They go online and post the breakdown, saying they're looking for someone to play a specific role. They give some of the basics, including a physical description and a general outline of the character's personality so that applicants who aren't a fit disqualify themselves before even submitting.

2. **Wait for responses** - They get thousands of submissions within the first 2-3 days of posting because so many actors are looking for work.

3. **Narrow them down as fast as possible** - They quickly sift through by looking at headshots and resumes and find that many of the responses they get are from people who have no idea what they are doing and should never be realistically considered. Why do they sift through so quickly? Because they don't have

time to look at so many different responses - they have a lot of other work to do.

4. **Look at reels and cover letters for the top 100-200 people** - The final 100-200 people they're left with will typically have their cover letters read (if they are shorter than 2-3 brief paragraphs), and they'll have their reels and/or websites checked. At this point, the casting director needs to ensure that the actors they're going to audition meet certain criteria, such as being highly talented and having a brand that fits the character they're auditioning for.

5. **Invite the top 50-100 actors to submit a self tape** - They now ask the actors to send something in that will give them an idea of whether the actor is qualified to come in for an actual audition. In some cases, this step might be skipped.

6. **Wait for responses** - Most actors will submit their self tapes within 12 hours. The people who take more than a day to respond are often cut - they're assumed to not be reliable.

7. **Review the self-tapes** - At this point, the casting director or their assistant will watch the self tapes to gauge whether the person is good enough for an in-person audition. It's usually too time-consuming to bring all those people in for real auditions, and they want to ensure they're professional and seem right for the role.

8. **Do the in-person auditions** - They'll usually bring in the top 20-30 people to audition in person. Why do they like to audition in-person? Because they need to meet the actors and see what they're like in real life. And that's *not* just to see how they respond to direction (although that's very important). Believe it or not, some people smell bad, some people don't have good manners or aren't friendly, some people are 10 minutes late to their audition, etc. They want to weed these people out and auditioning in-person makes it easy to do so.

9. **They make the final selection or host a callback** - A callback gives the casting director a chance to re-watch a couple final actors and compare them side by side. And they'll usually select the actor who most naturally fits the character, who seems to care the most about the project, who seems excited and interested to work on it, and who has fantastic acting skills.

Isn't it interesting that the "acting skills" was one of the last things in the list, yet most actors immediately think they need to work on their acting skills if they're not booking auditions. What about the other 90% on the list?

What Else Do Casting Directors Want?

Casting directors care about a lot when they're hiring, but not as much about the things you'd probably expect. For instance, they don't care if you make the right choice for how you play the character. And they don't care if your resume has some bigger credits than that of the actor who just walked in before you.

Number one on the list as we discussed is an actor who naturally fits the character they're auditioning for - both in personality and physical appearance. But beyond that, they also look for certain other traits we'll now cover.

If you can hit on each of the following points when you're sending out your cover letter and auditioning in-person, you'll be light years ahead of those who just hope they know what the casting director is looking for:

- **Make it easy** - Casting directors want someone who makes it easy for them to hire them. This all starts with the cover letter. Keeping your cover letter very short and readable while highlighting the two biggest benefits they'll get by hiring you is a good place to start. And then make it easy for them to audition you by showing up on time, being friendly, and showing them you're interested.

- **Be yourself** - Casting directors can always tell if you're putting on a fake personality to try to make them like you more. Just be yourself and be honest about whether you're right for a certain role or not. There's no point wasting your time submitting and auditioning for every role and every project. Remember the quote: *"He who* *trims himself to suit everyone will soon whittle himself away."*

- **Experience** - They want someone who knows a lot about the specific brand/type they are being hired to play.

- **Friendly** - They want someone who's nice and seems easy to work with. No one wants to work with a jerk and even if you're super talented, not being friendly will cost you the job over someone else who is more friendly.

- **Availability & neediness** - They want someone who is not too needy. If you can't make it to the initial audition, chances are they'll consider someone else over you, even if they offer to see you at a separate time. The more needy you seem, the less likely they will hire you because they'll feel like you're going to be more of a liability than an asset for the production.

- **Provides added value** - They want someone who is able to provide them even more value than they were expecting. If you have additional skills or personality traits that could be an asset to the project, they are often interested in knowing about them.

- **Cares about the role and project** - They want someone who really cares about the project and can explain why they want the job. They don't want you in a project if it's just for the money, because it means you won't do your best work. You have to really want it for the emotional reasons for them to bring you on.

- **Honest, reliable, and responsible** - They care about people who are honest and willing to be vulnerable. If you make a mistake and don't own up to it and apologize, but blame others, they will not hire you.

- **Emotionally stable** - Whenever I work as a casting director, I want to be sure that you're easy to work with. I have had actors in the past who were on an emotional rollercoaster, and it led to inappropriate outbursts on set and fights between cast and crew, which was bad for the production as a whole. Most casting directors want someone who is generally cool, collected, calm, and rolls with the punches.

What Do They Care About Most?

If I were to summarize everything into one all-encompassing statement, it would be this:

Casting directors want to hire someone who is naturally the character they're looking for, who is competent and easy to work with, and who will provide them with benefits, not features.

By benefits, I mean the following: they don't want you to tell them you know how to play the character type they're auditioning for really well. That is important, yes, but it is not the whole story. Why should they care? Why should they care you know how to play that character type? Everyone applying for the role should know how to play that character.

When you pitch yourself, explain the real benefits:

"As you can see from my reel, I'm very experienced playing this character type, so I'll fall into the role with minimal rehearsal time needed. It means I'll easily be able to take direction and will be ready from the get-go to start working with the cast. Because I'm a quick learner, I'll save the production time and money and I'll get the hang of it right away."

At the end of the day, when you're applying for a role, it all comes down to how you'll benefit the production or the person hiring you. If you want to earn more money or book bigger roles, always ask, "What's in it for them?" They don't care about your skills per-se. They care about what those skills mean for them.

Knocking the Audition Out of the Park

Did you know that agents know in the first 20 seconds or less of meeting an actor whether they are going to represent that actor? And did you also know that casting directors have a sixth sense as to who's going to get a callback just by how the actor walks into the room? Don't be one of the 80% of actors who don't get a second chance because of a silly mistake.

Here are a number of short tips to help you win over those with a critical eye.

1. Look Like a Million Bucks

You might think this is just a saying, but it's absolutely true. There is no way you are going to get a second chance if you walk in looking like a slob (unless the audition character calls for it). Nice, well-chosen clothes are a must if you want to have a successful acting career.

In addition to wearing good clothes, make sure you have clear, smooth skin, appropriate makeup & presentable hair. You should ALWAYS come into an audition looking just like the headshot you sent in (though you don't have to be wearing the same outfit).

Also, make sure that your hands are in good shape. No one likes to shake sweaty or extremely coarse hands.

2. Don't Chew Gum When You Come Into an Audition

Spit it out before entering the room, because chewing gum is impolite unless you brought enough for everybody. But do be sure your breath (and body) smells good. Bring some breath mints, and eat one right before entering.

Remember that the whole point is to give the casting director or agent absolutely no reason to hold anything against you.

3. When You Enter, Be Sure to Make Eye Contact

I can't tell you how many times I've had an actor come into an audition who wouldn't look me in the eye. It makes you appear untrustworthy and doesn't look professional. If you find it difficult to look someone in the eye when speaking to them, practice with your friends first.

4. Walk With Confidence, Holding Your Head High and Standing With Good Posture

Sit/stand up straight and lean forward a bit when listening to others, as it shows you are interested in what they have to say. If you lean back and sit/stand with bad posture, they will notice.

Be confident but not cocky. There is a difference between walking confidently and walking with a swag. If you do the latter, you are sure to get a negative reaction.

Let the casting director or agent know that you believe in your skills, but don't let them think you think you're better than everyone else.

5. Don't Shake Hands Unless They Offer Their Hand First

Germs and sickness makes everyone cautious these days. Therefore, be ready to shake the casting director or agent's hand if they offer it, but don't offer yours until they offer theirs.

If you do and they weren't planning on shaking your hand, they might feel uncomfortable, and you've just given them a reason to dislike something about you.

6. Never Forget to Bring a Copy of the Sides and Copies of Your Headshot/Resume

If you forget these things, you will seem irresponsible and not invested fully in their project. Be sure to also bring a copy of your acting reel on DVD and if you have one, a binder-style portfolio with photos just in case.

Have all of these things ready to pull right out of your bag. If you sit spending a few minutes trying to find what is needed in your bag, it puts a sour taste in the casting director or agent's mouth.

7. Invest in a Good Bag

Speaking of bags, having a nice, brand-name bag that is organized neatly and isn't dirty goes a long way in sending the message that you care about your career (and you're successful).

If your bag looks like a piece of junk, you will be judged. Remember: even though we live in a world where people aren't supposed to judge a book by its cover, almost everyone still does.

The honest and sad truth is that if you walk in with clothing or a bag that looks old and tattered or dirty, people will think you're irresponsible and don't care about what you do, or that you're not very successful in your acting career.

8. Treat Each of Those 20 Seconds Like Gold.

Remember that you have a purpose while you're there, so be sure that you use your time well. Speak with purpose and be clear in what you have to say.

No "um's," "whatever's," "like's," etc., as they make you look immature. Be polite, friendly, and confident.

9. Show Your Outgoing Personality and Answer Their Questions Clearly

People like to hear themselves talk, so the more you let the casting director do the talking, the more they will like you. If you just sit there talking about yourself the whole time, they won't like you very much.

But be sure to show your charisma and intelligence when they ask you a question. Research the production ahead of time so they can tell you did your homework. If they ask you a simple question and you don't know the answer, they will like you less.

But be truthful in your responses, and if you truthfully don't know an answer, tell them so. Don't try to make things up because it can get really awkward if they catch you.

10. A Brief, "Thank You for Seeing Me" When You Leave is a Great Way to Close the Audition

Be sure to ask them when you can expect to hear back, because you have a right to know. It not only shows you're interested in their project, but you'll also get access to information that you otherwise might not have known.

11. Arrive 5-10 Minutes Early

If you're even one minute late, it's over. You might as well not bother coming in because the immediate judgement will be, "Is this person going to show up on set late?"

They'll be worried you will cause production budget overruns, and in my honest opinion, there is absolutely no reasonable excuse to show up to an audition (or any job interview) late. You knew the time and could have planned way ahead for something this important.

All that being said, there is one possible way you can recover from coming in late, and that is by apologizing profusely, telling them why you were late, and then following up by saying you take full responsibility for making a bad decision and not planning ahead, and that you won't make that mistake again.

If you don't take responsibility and apologize, instead opting to blame other situations (no matter how dire), it will just look like you're unprofessional and don't want to take personal responsibility, which is a bad trait.

12. Try Looking the Part

This is something you'll want to test. Many filmmakers and casting directors are impressed when actors come in dressed similar to how they think the character would dress.

Doing this gets across two things: 1) You go above and beyond the call of duty, and 2) You already own the clothes they need so they won't have to rent clothing if they book you (this especially applies to things like cop uniforms and other specialty outfits).

All this being said, some casting directors get turned off if you come in dressed exactly as the character. So it's a toss up, but I always recommend giving it a shot because when you think about it, what's the worst that could happen? They won't book you.

13. Ask Questions During the Audition; Don't Just Talk About Yourself

By asking questions and showing interest in the production, you'll allow the casting director or filmmaker to talk about themselves and their role in the project.

As mentioned briefly earlier, the more you let them do the talking, the more they'll like and remember you. The best way to be interesting is... to be interested.

The more interested you are in them, the production, and their role in the project, the more interesting and engaging they'll find you, and chances are you'll get the callback.

14. Ensure You Have a Clear U.S.P. for the Production So They Need to Hire You

We discussed U.S.P. earlier in the book, so assuming you've been reading it through, this should already be taken care of. But if not, go back and visit Part 2.

What is it that you specifically can offer the production? What makes you different than everyone else coming into the room? In many cases, the best way to stand out from the crowd and have a clearly defined U.S.P. is by showing the casting director that you specialize in the type of character they are looking for and you have a strong, personal brand.

I hope this point has been driven home by now if you've been reading this book from the very beginning.

15. Under-Promise and Over-Deliver

If you really want to stand out at the audition, make sure to do some research on the production ahead of time because it will give you some ideas of how you might be able to contribute to the production beyond just acting.

Before you go into an important audition, think of at least two ways you could help the production beyond acting. Do you know someone who might be able to help them with locations and special access, or do you know someone who works in distribution who you can connect the director to?

For independent productions, directors and producers love to bring on actors who have more resources at their disposal than just their ability to act. What else can you bring to the table that will surprise and delight them?

Note: Do your homework. Don't just suggest things at random or you'll look desperate and it will come off as weird or inappropriate. Offer them something that they'll actually find useful.

16. Keep Your Cover Letter Short and Sweet, and Include One Unique Note In It

Actors frequently send me emails with cover letters that are either non-existent or two pages long with no paragraph breaks.

When someone goes out of their way to send me a very short, simple cover letter that covers why they are well-suited for the job, why they are excited to be a part of the production, and how they think they can help, I'm much more inclined to read it, meaning I'll probably remember you when you come in for the audition.

If you mention something unique and memorable in your cover letter and then bring that same thing up during your audition, the casting director might remember and it could be a great way to build rapport! This little trick can also increase your chances of being remembered later on when they are making their final decision.

17. Follow Up After the Audition

You'd be surprised at how many actors forget to follow up after an audition is over. Send a very short and simple 2-3 sentence note within 2-3 business days of the audition (or after they told you you would find out) to check in and say you were wondering if they had a chance to make a selection yet.

Keep your email short, simple, and friendly. Visit www.martinbentsen.com/get-cast to learn of a great resource I use to easily remember to follow up with people for free.

18. Eliminate Nervousness & Play to Your Brand

An easy way to get rid of nervousness before any audition is by saying your Pride Words in your head - the words you discovered in the earlier section on branding from Part 2.

If your brand is *the strong, compassionate, and loving father who can get violent at times*, you should always start by walking into the room replaying your Pride Words in your head. So say over and over again, *"I'm strong, compassionate, and loving. I'm strong, compassionate, and loving."* And really feel the emotions! You'll notice your nerves melt away completely.

Another way you can use your brand is by figuring out which aspects of your brand you'd like to focus on for this particular audition. Do you want to focus on *strong, compassionate, proud,* or *violent?*

You can even mix two words together to make the character multi-dimensional and more interesting. Such as, *"I'll play this character as both loving but violent,"* or *"I'll play it as strong but compassionate."*

By being specific, casting directors will take note and you'll be much more likely to get the callback. More on this in a moment.

19. Appreciate Their Criticism

We've discussed criticism previously in this book, but it's worth mentioning again. Have you ever received criticism and been annoyed by it? I know I have. But anyone giving your criticism, especially during an audition, is doing it because they hope it helps you change for the better.

Even if you completely disagree with their criticism, pretend you are super appreciative of it because it will make the person giving it feel special and smart. The best way to get someone to like you is to make them feel good, and anything you can do to make the casting director feel smart, special, appreciated, and happy is going to increase your chances of getting called back.

So next time you're at an audition, thank them for providing you the feedback (even if you disagree with it) and say that you really like their ideas on direction for the scene. Then perform it the new way and chances are, you'll have someone who strongly considers bringing you in again.

20. Ask The Five W's and H About Your Character Before Coming In

Making clear choices for your character before walking into the audition is extremely important. You'd be surprised at how many actors don't make clear choices before coming in!

In addition to fitting the character into your brand, you should also ask the Who, What, Where, When, Why, and How questions for every scene before you audition. The more specific you are with the choices you make, the better your performance will be.

This is crucial, especially when you don't know how the director will want you to play the character. Remember, making the wrong choice is infinitely better than making no choice at all - the casting director will just give you notes and you can try it differently.

So next time you're about to go in for an audition, ask the following:

- *Who* am I (the character) as a person?

- *When* and *Where* is this scene taking place? Has something just happened that might influence my behavior?

- *What* am I trying to achieve in this scene overall and also moment to moment?

- *Why* am I trying to achieve this goal?

- *How* am I going to achieve it, and *how* will I change my tactics throughout the scene?

If you apply all 20 of these tips, and you're applying to auditions you're right for, just think of how much work you'll soon be booking.

Start Connecting With People in the Industry

When I used to hear the word networking, immediately what came to mind was a bunch of old people with glasses of wine in some corporate office shaking each other's hands, passing out business cards, and trying to sell services to one another in a dishonest and sleazy way.

But the networking we're going to talk about is different. What you need to do is form connections with people at events, in classes, and even on set and then keep in touch with them.

- **Networking with actors** - This is just as important as networking with directors, agents and casting directors. Actors can connect you to agents, let you know of opportunities they hear about, and make recommendations for headshot photographers, web designers, and other service providers you might need down the line. But remember that it goes both ways. If you hear of a role for a look that you can't play (an older woman, if you're a young guy for instance), you can tell your actor friend about the role and recommend they check it out. They will feel grateful that you thought of them and they'll look for opportunities to help you out next time around.

- **Networking with directors & producers** - You can reach out to filmmakers and theater directors and keep in touch with them over time to eventually start bypassing casting directors. Look for filmmakers, producers, and theater directors who are creating unique and award-winning productions and show interest in their projects and cheer them on over the course of a few years. Then, the next time they're working on a new project, because you were so nice to them, they might invite you to audition!

- **Networking with casting directors and agents** - Going to classes and meeting casting directors and agents is another great way to connect with people. Many casting directors and agents are open to you occasionally sending them postcards or emails to let them know of new shows you're in (if you pay for their ticket & invite them to see the show). This type of networking often leads to audition opportunities or representation offers down the line. More on this in the next section.

Target Your Networking

We've talked about networking in general, but it's actually very important that you target your networking, just like you've been targeting the projects and roles you're right for. You don't want to just connect with people at random!

Since you're now clear on the types of projects you want to audition for, it's time to do a little research online. You're going to want to form relationships with casting directors (and directors, producers, agents, and actors) who are involved with those types of projects.

Search online for who is working on what (check out www.martinbentsen.com/get-cast for a great resource on how to find the most up-to-date information on castings), and then use Google to find out if the people you want to connect with are holding any seminars or events in the near future where you might be able to meet them in person.

Legitimate pay to play classes can be a great opportunity for you to network with people in the industry. Assuming your acting and auditioning technique is up to par, you'll be able to attend those classes for a small fee, and then when the class ends, you can ask the casting director or agent if they are open to you keeping in touch with them.

Ask them how they prefer to be contacted - email or postcards? They'll tell you the best method, and then you can set a reminder for yourself so you remember to follow up with them occasionally. After a bit of time, when they're casting for that project you want to be a part of, you can reach out and tell them you feel you'd be a perfect fit for the role, and you can ask if they're open to having you come in and audition for it.

Note: If a casting director tells you they don't want you to stay in touch, don't worry. Occasionally this happens, so just move on to someone else.

As a reminder, check out www.martinbentsen.com/get-cast to see a great free resource I recommend that will help you remember to follow up with people.

Make Contacts and Keep a Personal List

We covered this briefly earlier in the book, and now it's time to start using that list you created. If you didn't create your list, just go through all your old email contacts and compile a list of everyone's information, including name, email, and phone number. Keep this list and add to it every day as you come across more people you want to keep in touch with. Also note the date of the last contact with each person so it's easier to see who you haven't spoken to in a while.

Over time, you'll want to occasionally message these people (on average, once every three months) to see how things are going with them. Try to remember at least one special fact about them that stands out because it will touch them to know that you remembered.

Make sure you note the fact in your list. For instance, you can write: "Last contact - her husband was in the hospital." Then, three months later, you email her and ask how her husband is doing. Think of how she'll feel knowing you remembered!

Your list will continue to grow over the years and people will not forget who you are. Over time, you'll start to notice whether certain people really care about your relationship or not, and you'll be able to whittle down the list to just the most valuable contacts for you - the ones you care the most about the those who care about you the most.

Keeping a contact list and following up with people can truly change your career because it dramatically increases the chance of you being handed that once in a lifetime opportunity since you're always staying "top of mind" by following up with people.

Additionally, imagine things are going slowly, and you're not making much money from acting. If you need more work, you can just email out to all those directors you worked with in the past and say, "Hey, how have things been going? Have you been working on any new projects?" And they might wind up asking you to audition for something!

Part 6: Keep Moving Up

You've planned. You've created your basic marketing materials. You're auditioning and networking.

I'm proud of you for following through and sticking the course! Most people can't follow through on long-term strategies because it's so easy to get bogged down in tactics.

After just a year of auditioning and following what's outlined in this book, you should be booking up extremely well and be way ahead of most other actors who have been working for many years.

Now that your career is solidifying, it's time to turn your attention to your advanced marketing materials and look at a few final things that can take your acting career from great to phenomenal.

We'll be discussing your demo reel, actor website, and how to land a great agent or manager.

Shall we begin?

Create a Great Demo Reel

Funny how late in the game a serious demo reel is needed. We're already through 3/4 of this book and haven't discussed demo reels until now! Why?

Many actors think this is one of the first things they need (besides their headshot and resume), but you now know how much more important it is to figure out what you're right for first. While having footage of yourself performing is important, it's not going to do anything for you if it's not right for your brand and the projects you're targeting.

Chances are, by this point you've booked at least a few good projects and you're just waiting for your footage to be made available so you can download it and add it into your reel.

Casting directors like to see demo reels because they show the different projects you've acted in and give a sense of how good of an actor you actually are in different situations.

So, how do you create an effective demo reel?

It really boils down to two things: good samples and good editing. Hire an editor who can cut together a great reel for you, but be sure that you choose the best moments of your performances. The better the moments you choose, the better your reel will be.

Show a range... Don't just show the parts where you yell; show other stuff too, like where you cry. Show those moments where you really listen to the other actor and respond genuinely. And make sure the clips you choose are focused on showing different elements of your brand.

Note: I can't tell you how important it is that YOU choose the clips for your reel. If you dump hours of footage on an editor, they might just act lazy and choose clips to finish it fast, instead of spending all the time that's needed to pick out great clips. Also, how can you expect to the editor to know your brand as well as you do?

Here are a few things to note about demo reels:

- **Keep it short** - As a filmmaker who's been involved with the casting process many times, nothing bothers me more than when an actor sends me a reel that's more than two minutes. No matter who you are, even if your reel is entertaining, it should never ever be longer than two minutes. Ideally keep it to a minute and forty seconds. Put yourself in the casting director or agent's shoes. As busy as they are, would they care to spend more than a minute or two watching footage of someone they've never met before? If they wish the reel was longer, that means you'll get called in. But if it's too long, they'll get tired of you and you won't get the call.

- **Put your best footage first** - Most casting directors won't watch more than twenty seconds of a reel if it's not good, so you want to be sure that they see your best scene right away so they'll stay to watch the rest. Or you can put your most noteworthy scene - something from a well-known film or TV show.

- **Skip the montage** - Unless your montage shows some amazing filming quality and makes it look like you've been in big budget productions, there's no point to having one. And if you really must have one, don't let it be more than five or six seconds and put it at the end.

- **Add a quick slate** - Make sure your name and contact info, along with a headshot if possible, appear at the beginning and end of your reel. It should be there just in case someone comes across your reel without your contact information.

- **Cut scenes short** - Cut out segments of scenes that don't show you as much. You can remove portions of other actors talking, or shorten it to keep the focus on you. Essentially, you can re-edit scenes a bit to make it more about you than the other actor. Casting directors don't need the whole scene because they don't care about the story. They just want to see what you look and sound like on camera.

- **Show that you can act for screen** - Casting directors hate seeing theatrical acting on film. If you don't know how to act for film, learn how before making a reel (if you're making a reel for theatrical productions, don't worry about this as much). Also, ask your friends to be honest with you about your acting in the scenes you plan to use. Ask them for negative feedback, like what they didn't like about your acting technique. If they say anything negative that makes sense to you, rethink using that footage in your reel. Also, make sure whoever you hire to edit your reel tells you the truth too. You'll thank them later when the casting directors call you in.

- **Have at least one high-end professional scene in your reel -** To make a stronger impression, you want it to look like you've been a part of a bigger, more professional production. Even if you haven't been part of any high-end projects, we offer the option of doing an Actor Screener Shoot, where you can get a super high-end looking scene for an affordable price that features you as the main star. The scene is original, written for you specifically (see www.actorscreenershoot.com for more information). A high-end scene also tells casting directors you have experience working on professional sets.

- **Create reels for different types of work -** You should use a commercial reel for commercial submissions, a funny reel for comedy submissions, and a serious reel for dramatic submissions. But remember: you should primarily focus on one type of acting (your brand), being honest with yourself about what you should and should not play, and then develop a reel that supports that brand fully.

If you're interested in having a demo reel edited professionally (and you already have your footage or know where it's located online), visit www.demoreelsnyc.com.

Design Your Actor Website

A website is important, but not crucial to a successful acting career. I know many working actors who are booked solid and don't have a website!

But having a clean, professional site makes it easier for casting directors and anyone else to learn more about you, and it increases your professionalism in the eyes of others.

These days, most casting directors simply search the Internet to find out what they can on an actor before they decide to call them in. In fact, data shows that 92% of people in the hiring and casting process use social media to research applicants. Here's what they look for:

- Whether an actor has an online presence.

- Whether an actor has a significant social media following.

- Whether an actor has any additional footage beyond the demo reel they submitted.

- Whether an actor's IMDB or IBDB pages reflect what was on their resume.

- Whether there is anything posted online that gives them reason not to call the actor in (such as offensive social media postings or images).

- Whether an actor has his/her own website.

These days, you can easily design a professional-looking website for free using a drag & drop interface on numerous platforms. To see a listing of some tools I recommend for website creation, along with some actor websites you can model your own after, visit www.martinbentsen.com/get-cast.

Here are some things you should keep in mind when building your site:

- It should have a Welcome page, About page, Blog/Works page, Media page, Resume page, and Contact page.

- Make it visual and informative. Ask someone to check the grammar and spelling if you're not good at that yourself.

- Include on it your professional bio, headshot, resume, and reel, along with your phone number and email address. If you have an agent or manager, you can use their contact info instead.

- Make sure it's very easy to navigate and simple to understand (this is more important than you might realize).

- Include raves and reviews, especially if they are from someone noteworthy. We'll talk more about these in a moment.

- Include links that go directly to the websites of those you have worked with for projects - doing so gives you credibility.

- Use your blog as a place to post interesting commentary and photos of yourself working on projects with others.

- Allow people to comment on your blog and always respond to those comments quickly!

- Once designed, check your website on different computers and mobile devices to ensure it looks good everywhere! Also, be sure it loads quickly - no one wants to sit around for 5-10 full seconds waiting for your photos to load.

All this might sound daunting at first, but you can take your time with it. Spend a few hours designing your basic site and then you can set up a blog page later on. The most important thing is just getting your basic pages set up so next time you come to tackle it, most of the hard work will be done.

Note: Make sure all the links on your website are working properly. Always check them every few months because you never know if you accidentally deleted a page or something happened. If your links aren't working, you'll confuse your site visitors. Visit www.martinbentsen.com/ get-cast for some free resources I recommend that will allow you to check for broken links, page load time issues, and other important stats on your site.

Enhance Your Site with Reviews and Links

It's important for you to write down anything people say that really compliments your work, especially if someone famous or well-known said it. Put these quotes on your site and people who visit will instantly trust you more than the next actor, giving you a competitive advantage.

Also, be sure to link to public places where you appear. For instance, if you are on a TV show or online web series, link to those pages from your site and make sure people can click the link and watch them. Any time you say you were in something popular in your bio or elsewhere on your website, make it a clickable link right in the text. This lets people learn more about the project and trust that you aren't making things up.

Be sure to look for places where work or write-ups featuring you are posted online. If you see something written about you (you should be notified as things appear if you sent up your Google Alert as discussed earlier in the book), contact the website owner and request that they link back to your site.

If you see that the director of a production you worked on has posted a video with you online, contact him/her and ask if they will link to your website. Link building like this increases your ranking in Google and will increase the amount of people who can find you in the future for jobs.

The easiest way to find things posted about you is to both search your name in Google and search the websites of directors you have worked with in the past.

Just remember, it takes many months after you have finished working on a project for it to be posted online (sometimes even years), so you may need to wait awhile. If you want to remember to follow up, use the software I list at www.martinbentsen.com/get-cast to remind yourself to check on it six months or a year later.

Be sure to link to your "Internet Movie DataBase" (IMDB) or "Internet Broadway Database" (IBDB) pages. These are both great tools for you to build credibility and get more exposure. I also recommend paying for "IMDB Pro". It's not very expensive and gives you a lot more control of your profile so that you can keep your photos, clips, bio, and resume up to date. And remember, your IMDB and IBDB pages are verification tools casting directors can use to check that your resume credits are legit.

Land a Great Agent or Manager

If you really want to start booking consistent work, I recommend trying to get an agent or manager. They'll do their best to push for you to get more auditions, and they'll also have special access to roles you won't be able to find through online submissions websites, especially if you're focused on film and television work.

To help you find agents, I have a fantastic resource listed at www.martinbentsen.com/get-cast that contains the contact information of all the current agents in the industry.

Look for an agent or manager that would be a good fit for you and the types of roles you're interested in. Just like finding the right auditions, you want to carefully target the right agents instead of mass mailing everyone. Make a list of 10-15 agents/managers you think would be right for you.

Once you figure out who you want to meet, you can attend meet & greets or pay to play auditions and ask to keep in touch with them.

Check out www.martinbentsen.com/get-cast to watch an interview I did with well-known agent to learn how to land a talent agent and keep in touch with them effectively.

Remember that the more training and credits you have on your resume, the more likely an agent will take you on. They also love seeing strong reels.

When submitting to an agency, keep your cover letter short and to the point - it should be no more than 4-6 sentences, and should be specifically focused on why you're such a great fit for their specific agency. In general, the biggest reason actors don't hear back from agents is because their cover letter is too long or doesn't seem custom written, but rather reads like it was mass mailed to everyone.

I have a simple template that has been proven to get responses from agents, and has worked for many of my clients. Check it out at www.martinbentsen.com/get-cast.

Modify it as needed, but don't let it get any longer than it already is. Busy agents and managers don't have time to sift through tons of "Look at me!" rhetoric.

At a certain point in your career you're going to have to get an agent and/or manager to progress to the next level, but many actors try to get one before it's actually needed, which actually *hurts* them in the long run. If you skipped the rest of the book to read this section on agents, I'm talking to you!

The reason it can hurt you to get an agent too early is because if you sign with the wrong agency and they don't do a good job of submitting you, you'll be stuck with them for as long as your contract stipulates, and you'll also be stuck paying them an extra 10% of all your earnings. That can add up fast! You'll also be missing out on crucial negotiation experience, learning how contracts work, and general knowledge of the business side of acting.

Note: When looking for an agent or manager, remember that they work on commission. This means you should NEVER sign with an agent or manager who asks you to pay an up-front fee. They should also NEVER require you to get a headshot with a specific photographer (it's OK if they recommend certain photographers, but you should never feel forced into working with someone you don't want to - otherwise it's likely a scam.

Remember, since agents work on commission, they'll want to make sure you're a really good actor before they decide to bring you on and start submitting you. Their reputations are on the line, so why would they promote a bad actor?

Another important thing to keep in mind is that no one is going to come out of the blue and offer to represent you unless you somehow wind up in a huge production and they just so happen to see you and love it. But the chance of that happening is tiny.

It's your job to actively go out and pursue them yourself. And contrary to what most actors think, agents appreciate when you reach out to them with a good skillset and clear brand. It makes their job that much easier!

Besides finding agents at auditions or by sending cold emails, another way to get one is actually through an actor who already has one. This is another place where your contact list will come in handy. If you know someone with an agent, offer to buy them lunch or coffee and ask them how they got their agent and what they recommend you do to find an agent yourself.

Chances are they'll be open to making an introduction for you, and there's your chance!

Part 7: Be the Best

We've discussed a lot so far. We've covered how to get focused, how to get your marketing materials together, how to market and promote yourself, what goes into an effective audition, and even exactly what you need to do to get an agent or manager!

What have we not talked about?

Dare I say it? Social media.

Why have we not talked about that? Because it's not nearly as important as all these other things, and anyone who tries to sell you on social media marketing without asking you to get hyper focused, figure out what makes you different, and put together your basic marketing materials, is doing you a disservice.

Some actors spend years trying to build their Instagram following while ignoring the big wins in their career. The big wins include figuring out their brand and creating close connections to people in high places.

This is why social media is NOT something I will be covering in this book. Instead, in this final section, we are going to be discussing how you interact with people and how you present yourself to the industry. It's crucial to getting booked solid.

If you want to learn more about social media, check out www.martinbentsen.com/get-cast for some great info.

Customer Service & Going the Extra Mile

Let's talk about customer service. Customer service is very important to you, is it not? If you buy a $1,000 computer and the company just ignores you or gives you the run around when you have a problem and they won't let you return the computer, how would that make you feel?

The concept of going the extra mile means that as a service provider working as an actor, you should always be willing to go above and beyond to make the people you work with happy - agents, managers, directors, producers, and even other actors.

Think about it like this. If you were a director trying to manage everyone on set and having problem after problem and your actors all expected you to fully cater to their needs and wouldn't help you because they know it's not customary to do that, things would be normal.

But... imagine you're that same director and one of the actors offered to help out and was being really nice to you. How would that make you feel? You'd remember that actor and really want to keep in contact with them and spread their name around, right?

Another example: Imagine you're a busy agent and you're trying to submit your actors to all the projects you possibly can. What if one of your actors reached out to you and said they think they'd be perfect for a specific role that's available, and they sent you a pre-written cover letter that you could easily just slightly modify and submit?

Would you appreciate them for going above and beyond and helping you out? Will you be more likely to think of them and keep on top of their affairs more than those of some of the other actors you represent who just do the bare minimum?

If you go that extra mile to lend a helping hand (unless you are specifically asked not to), you will be remembered in the future. Your "customer service" of sorts will be so much better than that of most other actors, and it will be remembered and appreciated, and will come back to you in spades.

Your Body Must Match Your Brand

Think about your brand.

Does your body support it? Do you physically LOOK like the characters you're going out for?

Many actors focus on their training and auditions, but can forget about how they're presenting themselves to the world.

As an actor, your physical look is extremely important. You'll never be cast for a certain character type if you don't look like it - for instance, if you're a teenage guy, you'll never be able to play the role of an elderly grandmother.

Duh.

But although that example might sound obvious, there are more subtle versions of this as well - for instance, if you have crooked teeth you're less likely to get the part of a leading lady/man.

Unfair? Maybe. But true? You bet. Watch the interview I did with a well-known casting director if you don't believe me. You can see it at www.martinbentsen.com/get-cast.

Everything about your physical body combines together to create who you are, or your type.

So now I'd like to ask: is your body the way it should be to support the types you're going out for?

Go through the following checklist and see where you're letting things slip through the cracks! Be honest with yourself:

- **Haircut and style** - Is it supporting the characters and roles you're going out for?

- **Weight and fitness** - Is it supporting the characters and roles you're going out for?

- **Hygiene** - Is it helping or hurting your chances of connecting with people and networking?

- **Teeth** - Are they the way you want them? Are they supporting the characters and roles you're going out for?

- **Complexion** - Is your complexion supporting the characters and roles you're going out for?

- **Facial hair** - Is it supporting the characters and roles you're going out for?

- **Tattoos, jewelry, and makeup** - Are they supporting the characters and roles you're going out for?

- **Clothing style and colors** - Is it supporting the characters and roles you're going out for?

- **Your natural demeanor** - Do you act, talk, and sound like the characters you're going out for?

If you answered no to any of the above questions, then stop reading this book for a bit and get to work on making things the way they need to be. If you don't, your career will remain stuck!

No seriously, it will.

Casting directors (and anyone for that matter) are always making assumptions based on your appearance and how you interact with them.

If you've forgotten to check yourself for certain things before going to important auditions or meetings, your appearance is likely costing you opportunities.

Personality and Mindset is Important

Did you know that some of the things you say or do on a daily basis could be causing casting directors, agents, or other people in the industry to dislike you? You might not even be aware of them!

A sound mind is crucially important. As I hinted at earlier in this book, amazing actors often lose out to good actors when the good actor has a better personality.

Of course, my goal is for you to be both an amazing actor AND have an amazing personality, but when it comes down to it, your personality is slightly more important.

Why? Because people don't want to work with a jerk. If you're unpleasant to be around, you're unlikely to get very far in life.

"But wait!" you might say. "What about some famous celebrities who are complete a-holes?"

Well, most of the ones that are truly terrible were born into wealth and didn't have to work their way up. It's almost impossible to work your way up from the bottom if you've got a terrible personality.

So I'm going to present a short checklist of things to be aware of related to your personality. If you have any of these issues, I highly recommend speaking with a psychiatrist. Joking! I'll make some recommendations of a few great books to read that helped me with many of these issues. Be honest with yourself:

- Do you have the need to show people that you are very intelligent?

- Do you feel the need to help people even when they don't want your help?

- Do you judge others or talk about people behind their back?

- Do you try to prove to others how you're right or they're wrong?

- Do you let negative emotions cause you to say things that shouldn't be said?

- Do you avoid giving people the information they need or ask for in order to have an advantage over them?

- Do you not show enough appreciation for and gratitude to others?

- Do you claim credit for things that weren't your doing? Or do you claim too much credit instead of being humble?

- Do you accept full responsibility or make excuses when things go wrong?

- Do you treat some people unfairly without realizing it?

- Do you avoid apologizing when you're wrong?

- Do you sometimes not listen when people speak with you? Or do you focus on what your response is going to be instead of staying fully present to them?

- Do you attack people who are just trying to help you?

- Do you use your flaws as excuses for why you're not doing better?

If you're not sure, ask close friends or relatives to be honest and rank you from 1-10, with 10 being the worst, for each one of the above points.

If you're above a 4 for any of the above questions, you might want to consider asking yourself why you do that, and find out what you really get out of that behavior besides a good feeling in the moment. That behavior might just be what's holding you back!

If you haven't already, I highly recommend you check out these three fantastic books that can help immensely in developing a personality people really want to engage with:

1. **How to Win Friends and Influence People** (Dale Carnegie)

2. **What Got You Here Won't Get You There** (Marshall Goldsmith)

3. **Just Listen** (Mark Goulston)

Your Spirit Must Always Remain Positive

Sometimes, this industry gives us the most amazing levels of excitement and a feeling of aliveness you can't get anywhere else. And at other times, the rejection can feel like your soul is being ripped apart.

But what if there was a way to stay fulfilled and positive more easily? Is it even possible?

I believe it is, and it's all based on asking yourself a few key questions.

For this section, I'd like to reference something called "Human Needs Psychology," or the personal needs that every person supposedly has.

As some psychologists put it, there are six human needs:

1. **Certainty** - Everyone has the need for some level of certainty that they are OK and aren't about to lose everything. Without certainty, it's hard to function, so it's the first and most important need. An example would be that you're probably unlikely to perform well in an audition if you're uncertain where your next meal is coming from.

2. **Uncertainty and variety** - We all have the need for change and stimulation because without variety we'll get bored. An example is that you probably enjoy playing different types of characters and you'd get

bored auditioning for the same exact role days after day, year after year.

3. **Love and connection** - We all have a need to connect with other people in some way. Unless a person has a specific psychological disorder, everyone needs some sort of connection to other people, whether it's a romantic partner or just a friend.

4. **Significance** - We all have some sort of need to be different, special, or unique. If you feel too similar to everyone else, you'll lose your sense of self and won't feel like what you do matters. For certain people, they say, "Oh, I have no need to be unique, I'm spiritual." But isn't that their way of being unique?

5. **Growth** - We all have a need to move forward in some way and feel like we're progressing. If we're not getting better at something, we won't be happy.

6. **Contribution** - We all have a need to contribute and help people or society in some way, whether it's by sharing our ideas or just lending a helping hand.

It's important to realize that we will never be successful in our careers or lives at the level we want if we don't feel fulfilled and enjoy the work we do.

As the saying goes - if you love what you do, you'll never work a day in your life, right? Well, if you absolutely love acting, it will come easy and you'll get more and more opportunities.

But sometimes, we get overwhelmed, stressed, and down on ourselves if things aren't going our way.

Or we might need to do things like marketing that we don't necessarily love doing. And rather than do those difficult things, we decide to focus on the things we do love - like training or performing - and this lack of focusing on our marketing can hold us back.

So how do you get the feeling of fulfillment back and start loving what you're doing so you do it more passionately and perform at an even higher level?

By asking yourself the following six questions:

- From 1-10, what level of certainty do I have that I'm a great actor? What would I need to do to make that a 10?

- From 1-10, what level of variety and excitement do I have in my acting career? What could I do to make that a 10?

- From 1-10, what level of love & connection to others do I get when I act? What could I do to make that a 10?

- From 1-10, what level of significance do I get from acting? What needs to change to make that a 10?

- From 1-10, what level of growth do I get when I act? What could I do to make that a 10?

- From 1-10, what level of contribution do I feel when I'm acting? How could I make that a 10?

Come up with genuine answers to the above questions. Seriously, you might come up with some amazing ideas you'd have NEVER thought of otherwise, and these could be just what you need to take your acting career to the next level.

BONUS: If you want, try asking those same questions, but instead of focusing on acting in general, ask them specifically about marketing your acting career. You might come up with some brilliant solutions to make marketing yourself more enjoyable!

Get Away From Bad Situations & Take Charge of Your Life

I remember back in 2013, I was on the set of a feature film I was directing and it was 2am. Everyone was super tired and we had an early call time at 6:30am the next morning!

We were just about to wrap when I realized that the main actor had been wearing the wrong shirt for the entire scene.

We were working with a very limited budget and had no props and costume designer or coordinator, so it was easy to overlook such a small detail.

I looked at the actor and then pointed at my shirt. As the horrible realization dawned across his face, he let out a scream and took off, running into the woods.

Again, it was 2am.

I had no idea where he went, but I followed, and after about 5-10 minutes, I found him, laying on the ground crying and cursing to himself. It took a while to calm him down, and eventually we realized that we could edit around the mistake and chances were slim that the audience would notice.

Although it's a crazy story, things like that happen frequently in the film industry.

Throughout your career, you'll wind up in situations where you feel like you're about to go crazy and you want to scream. Relax and hold your tongue, or you could wind up saying or doing something that gets you blacklisted everywhere! The acting industry is much smaller than you think and you don't want an inappropriate outburst to cause people to badmouth you to their friends.

Now let's get one thing clear: I do NOT mean you should let people walk all over you. If there is something that doesn't feel right, you have to tell the person you are working with flat out that you cannot continue to work with them.

In some situations, it's better to stop working with people completely, even if they are paying you.

"Sometimes you have to pay to clean the sh** off your shoes."

This was something my father's friend used to tell him. It means sometimes you have to make a sacrifice before things can get better.

I've had to cut some paying headshot clients loose and never work with them again because of all the grief I had to put up with. It's the same with acting: you just have to quit some projects when you can't deal with them, even if they are paying fairly well.

I think one of the best examples of this is called the *Red Velvet Rope Policy*, an idea introduced by Michael Port in his best-selling book *Book Yourself Solid* (I highly recommend reading it).

Michael says, "You have to cut the bad clients loose and raise the bar for future clients."

Don't let certain people or projects past your red velvet rope. The amount of money and the amount of good work you'll get if you do this will rise dramatically over the course of the coming months.

Michael Port outlines these benefits:

1. You will be happier and seem more appealing to future employers and clients.

2. You won't have relationships that make you mutually unhappy, which will lead to less people badmouthing you in the future.

Remember, yelling or losing your cool is the easy way out of a situation, whereas keeping calm and working to make things right is the hard but better way. Work to build trust and you'll be memorable in the future.

Good word of mouth travels slowly in the entertainment industry. Bad word of mouth travels insanely fast, so you have to keep it to a minimum.

Why does bad word of mouth travel so quickly? Because people love drama. Bad word of mouth equals drama; and good word of mouth equals boring.

So next time you find yourself in a situation that is freaking you out and you don't know what to do, try to think about the facts...

Is it worth it to stay in this situation or will you be better off not being there? What is the risk of leaving? Once you know the risks, decide whether to leave or not. If you choose to leave the situation, do it professionally and don't yell and freak out. Just kindly say that you can't be involved anymore, and then you can leave and forfeit being paid.

But be sure that you're not violating your contract by leaving. You don't want to get sued!

And after you get out of the situation, make sure to take time to do some self-reflection.

There's a great book called *The Success Principles* by Jack Canfield (which I also highly recommend). It talks all about blame and taking personal responsibility for all things that happen to us.

He recommends asking the following question when things go wrong:

How did I cause this to happen?

Typically when something goes wrong (like fights and other crazy things on set), we all have the immediate urge to point the finger and say it wasn't our fault.

How could I have known the people on set would be difficult to work with and the director would be a terrible person? I definitely didn't cause this to happen, right?

Well, the book says that by consistently asking how we cause the things around us to happen, we'll start to gain an unconscious feeling of control that gives us more power over everything in our lives.

It also says that the more we blame and point the finger, the more we'll stay stuck.

Was it truly your fault that you got involved with a set like that? Maybe, maybe not.

Perhaps you could have done some research ahead of time on the cast and crew to see who you'd be working with and what other people were saying about them. Perhaps you could have left sooner, like when you first started seeing red flags - instead of waiting until the situation deteriorated so much.

Well, if you really did create that situation, it means you'll be unlikely to let something like that happen again. In the future, you can do extra research to ensure the productions you're joining are legit and have good people with lots of credits to their names.

The key takeaway here is that we can choose to either blame others and let our setbacks disappoint us or we can take full responsibility for everything in our lives and extract as much value out of our setbacks as possible.

So the next time you face a challenge or hurdle in your acting career, I'd like you to ask yourself the following three questions and come up with real answers:

1. How did I create this situation?

2. Will feeling the way I feel right now help me fix this situation or will it keep me stuck?"

3. How can I use this situation to my advantage? (my personal favorite)

If you do that consistently whenever things get difficult - nothing can possibly hold you back.

Stay Confident & Believe in Yourself

The world we live in gives opportunities to people who already have a lot of success. This is because people who appear successful are likely to be reliable, trustworthy, and deserving of more things. Therefore, people who appear very confident in what they do will be more likely to get hired for the job.

So stay confident and make sure it shows, even when things get difficult. If you appear confident, people will think you'll do a better job, and they will give you a chance.

Your headshot is the first step in deciding whether to cast you. Next is your resume. Then your cover letter and reel. And finally your audition and personality. If you can make your confidence show in all of these steps (without seeming cocky), you'll have a much better chance in the acting world.

No one can do the things that need to be done but you, and actors only fail when they stop believing in themselves.

As I mentioned in the foreword to this book, I'm not interested in tactics. Social media, mailing lists, and all those other random ideas some people teach are not going to lead you to success.

What will lead you to success is planning, strategizing, putting in consistent, focused effort, not being afraid to ask for opportunities, and most of all, not giving up.

A great acting career is NOT built on great talent.

A great acting career is NOT built on "who you know."

A great acting career is built on a solid foundation of focus and slow, thoughtful planting of seeds and consistent watering and caring for them over the years.

One day the people around you will look up and go, "When did that tree get so big?"

If you believe that you're a great actor (and you should) and you want to reach the success you deserve, then you must take action to earn it.

As an actor, it's your job to first work as a service provider and give people what they want. And after you've paid your dues, after you've spent many years of your life listening to the world, the world will be ready to listen to the artist in you.

Although you've reached the end of this book, think of it as the very beginning. It's time to start putting in the effort to make things happen.

If you're already moving your career forward and seeing success, I recommend going back to the beginning and re-reading this any time you get stuck. At each level of your acting career, you're going to find new insights and each chapter will hold new meaning and help guide you to that next level.

And if you haven't already, I highly recommend visiting www.martinbentsen.com/get-cast to access the bonus resources and take all the information in this book to an even deeper level.

Conclusion

Now that you have read through this book, I ask you...

Have you started doing anything?

Nothing is going to change in your acting career if you don't start putting these tips into use. Many people buy books like these, go through them with a highlighter, but then never come back to them to turn the paper highlights into real life highlights.

Nothing is going to change without you putting in the effort and making the changes. Doesn't the world deserve to hear your voice?

So go out there and make it happen!

I hope to one day have the opportunity to meet you personally and see how far you've come.

Sincerely,

Martin Bentsen

Actor Marketing Coach

www.martinbentsen.com

Made in the USA
Middletown, DE
28 February 2020